# Introduction
# to Crochet

# Introduction to Crochet

## Beginner–friendly patterns for wreaths, decorations, and home accessories

## Kate Eastwood

CICO BOOKS

LONDON NEW YORK

♥ To all the crocheters who have inspired and encouraged me along the way ♥

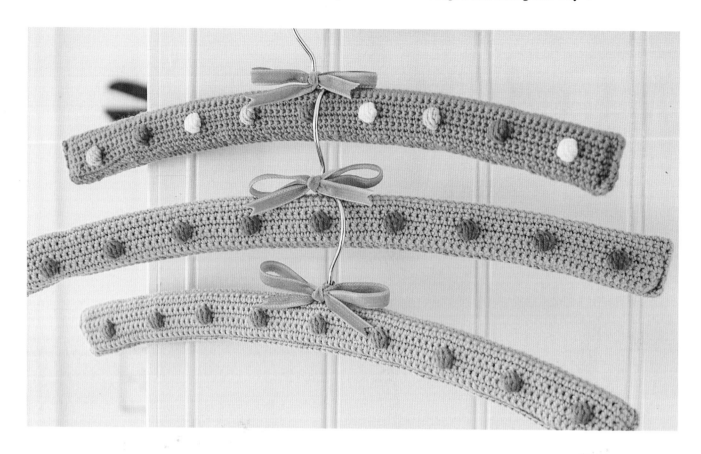

Published in 2024 by CICO Books
an imprint of Ryland Peters & Small Ltd
341 E 116th St, New York, NY 10029

www.rylandpeters.com

10 9 8 7 6 5 4 3 2 1

Text © Kate Eastwood 2024
Design, illustration, and photography © CICO Books 2024

The designs on pages 16–33, 44–59, and 64–77 have
previously appeared in *Crocheted Home* and *Crocheted
Wreaths & Garlands* by Kate Eastwood.

A CIP catalog record for this book is available from
the Library of Congress.

ISBN: 978 1 80065 314 6

Printed in China

Editor: Marie Clayton
Pattern checker: Jemima Bicknell
Designer: Alison Fenton
Photographers: James Gardiner and Emma Mitchell
Stylist: Nel Haynes
Illustrator: Stephen Dew

Editor: Jenny Dye
Art director: Sally Powell
Creative director: Leslie Harrington
Head of production: Patricia Harrington
Publishing manager: Carmel Edmonds

# Contents

Introduction 6

# Introduction

I am so pleased to have had the opportunity to put this book together, as I hope that it will be the starting point for others to get as hooked on crochet as I am! I will never be able to sing the praises loudly enough of the pleasure that crochet has brought to my life.

Little did I know when I tentatively started to teach myself to crochet by watching YouTube videos a few years back, that it would become such a big part of my day-to-day life. I can honestly say that it is very rare for me to have a day when I don't crochet. Not only is it the most amazing feeling to look at a finished project and know that you have created something simply from a hook and some yarn, but for me the mindfulness that comes with concentrating on each piece is now a big part of how I wind down at the end of the day.

Having always been a knitter, I found that I was drawn to crochet projects that were a little different to the stereotypical granny-square style of crochet, where the crochet has more of a "knitted," solid texture. I also love the look of a project that has been worked purely in single crochet (UK double crochet) stitch, so many of my designs are mostly made up of this one simple stitch.

The projects I have created and selected for this collection are simple to make but look colorful and detailed, all while being mainly worked in single crochet. If you are yet to learn to crochet or are relatively new to the craft, I hope that my book will inspire you to take your crochet to the next level, and that you will find the whole process, from start to finish, as enriching and enjoyable as I do.

## Before you begin

If you are a beginner or come across a technique or term you don't understand, please check out the techniques section on pages 78–93 and the abbreviations list on page 94. Each of the projects has a skill rating—Very Easy (one circle), Easy (two circles), or Intermediate (three circles). Start with the Very Easy projects, then move on to the next two levels once you have got to know the basic techniques.

# CHAPTER 1
# Home Accessories

# Trio of storage baskets

These baskets will neaten any bathroom, desk, or craft room. Made in three different sizes they can be used for all your odds and ends. They are crocheted using two strands of coordinating colored cotton, with one of the colors being chosen for the finishing band around the top of each basket. With a square of crochet as the base, the sides are worked in a simple continuous round, making this an easy make with very little counting or place marking needed.

## SKILL LEVEL ● ●

### Yarn and materials
Rico Design Creative Cotton Aran (100% cotton, 93yd/85m per 1¾oz/50g ball) worsted (aran) weight yarn:
 5 balls in each of:
 Smokey Pink shade 06 (A)
 Saffron shade 26 (B)

### Hook and equipment
US size E/4 (3.5mm) crochet hook

Yarn needle

### Finished measurements
Large basket: 4¾ x 4¾ x 4¾in (12 x 12 x 12cm)

Medium basket: 4 x 4 x 4in (10 x 10 x 10cm)

Small basket: 3¼ x 3¼ x 3¼in (8 x 8 x 8cm)

### Gauge (tension)
15 sts x 16 rows = 4in (10cm) square working single crochet with 2 strands of yarn held tog, using a US size E/4 (3.5mm) crochet hook.

### Abbreviations
See page 94.

## Large basket

### BASE
Using one strand of A and one strand of B held tog, ch16 loosely.
**Row 1:** 1sc in second ch from hook and in each ch to end, turn. *(15 sts)*
**Rows 2–14:** Ch1 (does not count as st throughout), 1sc in each st to end, turn.
**Row 15:** Ch1, 1sc in each st to last st, (1sc, ch1, 1sc) in last st, do not turn.

### EDGING
**Round 1:** 1sc in each row end down left-hand side to last st, (1sc, ch1, 1sc) in last st, 1sc in each st along bottom edge to last st, (1sc, ch1, 1sc) in last st, 1sc in each row end up right-hand side to last st, (1sc, ch1, 1sc) in last st, sl st in start of top edge to join.
Fasten off.

## SIDES
**Round 1:** With RS facing, join in A and B held tog at one corner with a sl st, 1sc BLO in same st, 1sc BLO in each st around.
Work in a continuous spiral. PM in last st and move up as each round is finished.
**Rounds 2–19:** 1sc in each st around. At end of Round 19, sl st in first st to join.
Fasten off and sew in ends (see page 87).
**Round 20:** Turn to work from inside of basket, join in 2 strands of A at one corner with a sl st, 1sc in same st, 1sc in each st around.
**Rounds 21–27:** 1sc in each st around. At end of Round 27, sl st in first st to join.
**Round 28:** Ch1, work crab st as foll: working from left to right with RS facing (insert hook from back to front, work 1sc in next st to right) to end of round, sl st in top of ch-1 to join.
Fasten off.

## Medium basket

### BASE

Using one strand of A and one strand of B held tog, ch13 loosely.

**Row 1:** 1sc in second ch from hook and in each ch to end, turn. *(12 sts)*

**Rows 2–10:** Ch1 (does not count as st throughout), 1sc in each st to end, turn.

**Row 11:** Ch1, 1sc in each st to last st, (1sc, ch1, 1sc) in last st, do not turn.

### EDGING

**Round 1:** 1sc in each row end down left-hand side to last st, (1sc, ch1, 1sc) in last st, 1sc in each st along bottom edge to last st, (1sc, ch1, 1sc) in last st, 1sc in each row end up right-hand side to last st, (1sc, ch1, 1sc) in last st, sl st in start of top edge to join.

### SIDES

**Round 1:** With RS facing, join in A and B held tog at one corner with a sl st, 1sc BLO in same st, 1sc BLO in each st around.

Work in a continuous spiral. PM in last st and move up as each round is finished.

**Rounds 2–15:** 1sc in each st around.

At end of Round 15, sl st in first st to join.

Fasten off and sew in ends.

**Round 16:** Turn to work from inside of basket, join in 2 strands of B at one corner with a sl st, 1sc in same st, 1sc in each st around.

**Rounds 17–21:** 1sc in each st around.

At end of Round 21, sl st in first st to join.

**Round 22:** Ch1, work crab st as foll: working from left to right with RS facing (insert hook from back to front, work 1sc in next st to right) to end of round, sl st in top of ch-1 to join.

Fasten off.

## Small basket

### BASE

Using one strand of A and one strand of B held tog, ch11 loosely.

**Row 1:** 1sc in second ch from hook and in each ch to end, turn. *(10 sts)*

**Rows 2–8:** Ch1 (does not count as st throughout), 1sc in each st to end, turn.

**Row 9:** Ch1, 1sc in each st to last st, (1sc, ch1, 1sc) in last st, do not turn.

### EDGING

**Round 1:** 1sc in each row end down left-hand side to last st, (1sc, ch1, 1sc) in last st, 1sc in each st along bottom edge to last st, (1sc, ch1, 1sc) in last st, 1sc in each row end up right-hand side to last st, (1sc, ch1, 1sc) in last st, sl st in start of top edge to join.

### SIDES

**Round 1:** With RS facing, join in A and B held tog at one corner with a sl st, 1sc BLO in same st, 1sc BLO in each st around.

Work in a continuous spiral. PM in last st and move up as each round is finished.

**Rounds 2–11:** 1sc in each st around.

At end of Round 11, sl st in first st to join.

Fasten off and sew in ends.

**Round 12:** Turn to work from inside of basket, join in 2 strands of A at one corner with a sl st, 1sc in same st, 1sc in each st around.

**Rounds 13–16:** 1sc in each st around.

At end of Round 16, sl st in first st to join.

**Round 17:** Ch1, work crab st as foll: working from left to right with RS facing (insert hook from back to front, work 1sc in next st to right) to end of round, sl st in top of ch-1 to join.

Fasten off.

### Making up and finishing

Sew in all ends.

Fold the top edge of the basket over so that the single color band forms the finished edge.

# Daisy tote

This versatile tote has a multitude of uses, from yarn storage to gym bag, to swim bag to shopping bag. The choice is yours! Crocheted in a jersey ribbon on a medium-sized hook, it crochets up to give a soft but tough, roomy bag that will keep its shape well. The handles in this pattern have been made long enough for both a hand hold and to go over the shoulder, but the pattern can easily be adjusted to suit whichever you prefer.

## SKILL LEVEL ●

### Yarn and materials
Hoooked Ribbon XL (80% cotton, 20% other, 131yd/120m per 8¾oz/250g ball) bulky (chunky) weight yarn:
   4 balls of Spicy Ocre (A)
   1 ball of Pearl White (B)

### Hooks and equipment
US size J/10 (6mm) and US size H/8 (5mm) crochet hooks

Stitch marker

Large yarn needle

### Finished measurements
Bag: 20in (51cm) wide x 13¾in (35cm) high

Handle finished length: 17¾in (45cm)

### Gauge (tension)
11 sts x 12 rows = 4in (10cm) square working single crochet, using a US size J/10 (6mm) crochet hook.

### Abbreviations
See page 94.

## Bag body
Using US size J/10 (6mm) hook and A, ch45 loosely.
**Row 1:** 1sc in second ch from hook and in each ch to end, turn. *(44 sts)*
**Row 2:** Ch1 (does not count as st throughout), 1sc in each st to end, turn.
Rep Row 2 until work measures 26in (66cm), do not turn.

### EDGING
Ch2, 1sc in same st as last st of final body row, 1sc in each row end down left-hand side to last st, (1sc, ch2, 1sc) in last st, 1sc in each st along bottom edge to last st, (1sc, ch2, 1sc) in last st, 1sc in each row end up right-hand side to last st, 1sc in last st (same place as first st of final body row), ch2, sl st in start of top edge to join.
Fasten off and sew in ends (see page 87).

## Handles
(make 2)
Using US size H/8 (5mm) hook and B, ch101.
**Row 1:** 1sc in second ch from hook and in each ch to end, turn. *(100 sts)*
Fasten off B.
**Row 2:** Join in A, ch1, 1sc in each st to end, turn.
Fasten off A.
**Row 3:** Join in B, ch1, 1sc in each st to end, turn.
Fasten off and sew in ends.

## Making up and finishing
With RS facing, fold bag in half from top to bottom.

### JOINING
Using US size H/8 (5mm) hook, join in A at top of left-hand side with a sl st, 1sc in same st, 1sc in each row end through both layers to bottom of bag. Fasten off.
Using US size H/8 (5mm) hook, join A at bottom right-hand corner with a sl st, 1sc in same st, 1sc in each row end through both layers to top of bag. Fasten off.

### TOP EDGING
**Round 1:** Using US size H/8 (5mm) hook, join in B at top edge, 1sc in each st all around opening, sl st in first st to join.
**Round 2:** Ch1, work crab st as foll: working from left to right with RS facing (insert hook from back to front, work 1sc in next st to right) to end of round, sl st in top of ch-1 to join. Fasten off.

### SIDE EDGING
**Row 1:** With RS facing, using US size H/8 (5mm) hook and B, work crab st along each side. Fasten off.

## ATTACHING HANDLES

Lay the finished bag on a flat surface. Count in 13 sts from one side and 3 rows down from the bottom of the white edge. Mark this point. Working from the inside of the bag, thread one end of one of the straps through to the front of the bag. Pull enough of the strap through to enable you to tie a firm knot.

Count in 13 sts from the other side and 3 rows down as before and attach the other end of the strap in the same way. Turn the bag over and repeat to add the other handle.

Using a length of B in a yarn needle sew a daisy onto the front of the bag with lazy daisy stitches (see page 90). Use a small amount of either A or B to work a French knot (see page 90) as the center of the daisy.

# Circular placemats

These mats are so quick and easy to make that in no time at all you can add a fresh new look to your dining table.

## SKILL LEVEL ●

### Yarn and materials

*For two mats:*
Hoooked Zpagetti Solid (90% cotton, 10% other, 131yd/120m per 24½oz/700g ball) super bulky (super chunky) weight yarn:
  1 ball of Off White shade 28 (A)

Cascade Yarns Noble Cotton (100% cotton, 220yd/201m per 3½oz/100g ball) light worsted (DK) weight yarn:
  1 ball of Pale Gold shade 15 (B)

### Hooks and equipment

US size J/10 (6mm) and US size E/4 (3.5mm) crochet hooks

Stitch marker

Yarn needle

### Finished measurements

10½in (27cm) diameter

### Gauge (tension)

10 sts x 10 rows = 4 x 3¾in (10 x 9.5cm) working single crochet, using a US size J/10 (6mm) crochet hook and Hoooked Zpagetti Solid.

15 sts x 15 rows = 2¾ x 2½in (7 x 6.5cm) working single crochet, using a US size E/4 (3.5mm) crochet hook and Cascade Yarns Noble Cotton.

### Abbreviations

See page 94.

### Special abbreviation

**MB loop (make bobble loop):** [yarn over hook, insert hook in st, yarn over hook, pull through st as if starting a hdc, pull loop up to hdc height] 5 times all in the same st, leaving all loops on hook, yarn over hook and pull through all loops on hook, ch1

## Placemat

Using US size J/10 (6mm) hook and A, make a magic ring.
Work in a continuous spiral. PM in last st and move up as each round is finished.
**Round 1:** 6sc in ring. *(6 sts)*
**Round 2:** 2sc in each st to end. *(12 sts)*
**Round 3:** [1sc in next st, 2sc in next st] 6 times. *(18 sts)*
**Round 4:** 1sc in first st, 2sc in next st, [1sc in each of next 2 sts, 2sc in next st] 5 times, 1sc in last st. *(24 sts)*
**Round 5:** [1sc in each of next 3 sts, 2sc in next st] 6 times. *(30 sts)*
**Round 6:** 1sc in each of first 2 sts, 2sc in next st, [1sc in each of next 4 sts, 2sc in next st] 5 times, 1sc in each of last 2 sts. *(36 sts)*
**Round 7:** [1sc in each of next 5 sts, 2sc in next st] 6 times. *(42 sts)*
**Round 8:** 1sc in each of first 3 sts, 2sc in next st, [1sc in each of next 6 sts, 2sc in next st] 5 times, 1sc in each of last 3 sts. *(48 sts)*
**Round 9:** [1sc in each of next 7 sts, 2sc in next st] 6 times. *(54 sts)*
**Round 10:** 1sc in each of first 4 sts, 2sc in next st, [1sc in each of next 8 sts, 2sc in next st] 5 times, 1sc in each of last 4 sts. *(60 sts)*
**Round 11:** [1sc in each of next 9 sts, 2sc in next st] 6 times. *(66 sts)*
**Round 12:** 1sc in each of first 5 sts, 2sc in next st, [1sc in each of next 10 sts, 2sc in next st] 5 times, 1sc in each of last 5 sts. *(72 sts)*
**Round 13:** [1sc in each of next 11 sts, 2sc in next st) 6 times, sl st in top of first sc to join. *(78 sts)*
Fasten off.

## EDGING

Using US size E/4 (3.5mm) hook, join B in any st.
**Round 1:** 2sc BLO in each st to end, sl st in top of first sc to join, turn. *(156 sts)*
**Round 2 (WS):** Ch1 (counts as first st), sl st in next st, *MB loop in next st, sl st in each of next 2 sts; rep from * around edge of placemat, sl st in top of ch-1 to join.
Fasten off.

## Making up and finishing

Sew in any ends (see page 87).

# Cotton facecloths

These simple cotton facecloths will add a lovely homey touch to your bathroom and can be easily color coordinated by matching the border shade to your décor. Worked in seed (moss) stitch they have a soft textured feel—and since they are made in 100% cotton they are fully washable.

## SKILL LEVEL ●

### Yarn and materials

Debbie Bliss Eco Baby (100% cotton, 137yd/125m per 1¾oz/50g ball) sport (5-ply) weight yarn:
For one facecloth:
    2 balls of White shade 001 (A)
    1 ball of either Rose shade 012 (B)
    or Duck Egg shade 008 (C)

Approx. 6in (15cm) length of cotton tape per facecloth

### Hook and equipment

US size E/4 (3.5mm) crochet hook

Yarn needle

Sewing needle and thread

### Finished measurements

Approx. 12 x 10½in (30 x 27cm)

### Gauge (tension)

14 sts x 13 rows = 2½ x 3in (6.5 x 7.5cm) working pattern, using a US size E/4 (3.5mm) crochet hook.

### Abbreviations

See page 94.

## Facecloth

Using US size E/4 (3.5mm) hook and A, ch59.
**Row 1:** 1sc in second ch from hook, *1dc in next ch, 1sc in next ch; rep from * to last st, 1dc in last st, turn. *(58 sts)*
**Row 2:** Ch1 (does not count as st), 1sc in first st, *1dc in next st, 1sc in next st; rep from * to end of row, working 1dc in last st, turn. *(58 sts)*
Rep Row 2 until facecloth measures 11½in (29cm).
Fasten off.

### BORDER

**Round 1:** With RS facing, join A in top right-hand corner of facecloth, work 1sc in each st along top edge to corner, 2sc in corner st, 1sc in each row end down left-hand side, 2sc in corner st, 1sc in each st along bottom edge, 2sc in corner st, 1sc in each row end up right-hand side, 2sc in corner st, sl st in top of first sc to join.
Fasten off A.

**Round 2:** With RS facing, join either B or C in top right-hand corner, [1sc BLO in each st to corner, 2sc in corner st] 4 times, sl st in top of first st to join, ch1.
**Round 3:** Ch1 (does not count as st), *sl st in next st, ch1, sl st in next st, ch1; rep from * around entire edge of facecloth, sl st in top of first st to join.
Fasten off.

## Making up and finishing

Sew in ends (see page 87).
Fold length of cotton tape to make a loop and stitch this into place at one corner of the facecloth.

---

**TIP** For a perfect handmade gift work up one or two facecloths, add a bar of sweet-smelling soap, and tie up with some matching ribbon.

# Bobbly hanger covers

There's something a little bit luxurious about a covered hanger but with this super-easy bobbly version, all of your hangers can be given the star treatment! The covers and bobbles can be made in any color combination of your choice.

**SKILL LEVEL** ●

### Yarn and materials
Debbie Bliss Baby Cashmerino
(55% wool, 33% acrylic, 12% cashmere,
137yd/125m per 1¾oz/50g ball)
sport (5-ply) weight yarn:
   2 balls of Camel shade 102 (A)
   1 ball of Mustard shade 316 (B)
   Part ball each of:
   Flame shade 306 (C)
   White shade 100 (D)

### Note
Yarn quantitites given are to make the hanger covers shown. If you want to switch colors, each cover requires one ball of the main color and a part ball for the bobbles.

10in (25cm) of ½in (1cm) wide coordinating ribbon per hanger

3 wooden hangers, 17¼in (44cm) long

### Hook and equipment
US size E/4 (3.5mm) crochet hook

Yarn needle

### Finished measurements
Width 17¼in (44cm), circumference 3½in (9cm)

### Gauge (tension)
15 sts x 15 rows = 2½ x 2⅜in (6.5 x 6cm) working single crochet, using a US size E/4 (3.5mm) crochet hook.

### Abbreviations
See page 94.

### Special abbreviation
**MB (make bobble):** using yarn that is laid along top of row, [yarn over hook, insert hook in stitch, yarn over hook, pull yarn through work, yarn over hook, pull yarn through first 2 loops on hook] 6 times all in same stitch, using main color yarn over hook, pull through all loops on hook

## Cover
Using US size E/4 (3.5mm) hook and A or B, ch94.
**Row 1 (RS):** 1sc in second ch from hook, 1sc in each ch to end, turn. *(93 sts)*
**Rows 2–4:** Ch1 (does not count as st throughout), 1sc in each st to end, turn.
**Row 5:** Ch1 in main color, lay second color of your choice along top of row, 1sc in main color in each of next 6 sts (working over second color), MB in second color, *1sc in main color in each of next 9 sts, MB in second color; rep from * to last 6 sts, 1sc in each of last 6 sts, fasten off second color, turn.
**Rows 6–14:** Ch1, 1sc in each st to end, turn. *(93 sts)*
**Row 15:** Rep Row 5.
**Rows 16–19:** Ch1, 1sc in each st to end, turn. *(93 sts)*
Fasten off.

## Making up and finishing
Find the central point of the cover by folding it in half lengthwise and widthwise. Push the hanger hook through the center point. Shape the cover around the hanger. Using the main color yarn, work a sc seam down each of the short edges and along the bottom of the hanger to join the cover front to the cover back. Fasten off and sew in any ends (see page 87). Add a coordinating color ribbon and tie in a bow at the base of the hanger hook.

# Dish towel edging

**To add the prettiest of touches to a dish towel, crochet this simple bobbly edging in cotton yarn along the top and bottom edges of the cloth. This can be worked in any number of color combinations.**

## SKILL LEVEL ●

### Yarn and materials

Cascade Yarns Ultra Pima (100% cotton, 219yd/200m per 3½oz/100g ball) light worsted (DK) weight yarn:
  1 ball of Sage shade 3720 (A)

Cascade Yarns Noble Cotton (100% cotton, 220yd/201m per 3½oz/100g ball) light worsted (DK) weight yarn:
  1 ball of Pale Gold shade 15 (B)

2 dish towels (any size)

### Hook and equipment

US size B/1–C/2 (2.5mm) crochet hook

Sewing needle with large eye

Yarn needle

### Finished measurements

Edging: approx. ½in (1.5cm) wide

### Gauge (tension)

15 sts x 15 rows = 2½ x 2⅜in (6.5 x 6cm) working single crochet, using a US size B/1–C/2 (2.5mm) crochet hook and Cascade Ultra Pima.

15 sts x 15 rows = 2½ x 2⅜in (6.5 x 6cm) working single crochet, using a US size B/1–C/2 (2.5mm) crochet hook and Cascade Yarns Noble Cotton.

### Abbreviations

See page 94.

### Special abbreviation

**MB loop (make bobble loop):** [yarn over hook, insert hook in st, yarn over hook, pull through st as if starting a hdc, pull loop up to hdc height] 5 times all in the same st, leaving all loops on hook, yarn over hook and pull through all loops on hook, ch1

### Edging

Using the sewing needle threaded with A or B, sew a line of blanket stitch along the top and bottom edges of thedish towel, spacing stitches approx. ¼in (0.5cm) apart and ending with an even number of sts.
Using a US size B/1–C/2 (2.5mm) hook and A or B, with RS of dish towel facing, join yarn at right-hand corner of stitched edge.
**Row 1:** *1sc in first st, 2sc in next st; rep from * to end of row.
Fasten off first color.
**Row 2:** With RS facing, join any color at right-hand corner, 1sc BLO in each st to end. Fasten off.

**Row 3:** With RS facing, join any color at right-hand corner, *sl st BLO in next st, MB loop BLO in next st, sl st BLO in next st; rep from * to end. Fasten off.

### Making up and finishing

Sew in any ends (see page 87).

**TIP** This would make the perfect holiday gift if you worked the edging onto a festive dish towel.

# Coffee table coaster set

**Add a little color to your coffee table with these cheery coasters. When not in use they can be stacked up in the matching basket to keep them tidied away.**

**SKILL LEVEL** ●

## Yarn and materials

Wool and the Gang Shiny Happy Cotton (100% cotton, 155yd/142m per 3½oz/100g ball) worsted (aran) weight yarn:
    1 ball of Eucalyptus Green (A)
    1 ball of True Blood Red (B)

Rowan Cotton Glacé (100% cotton, 126yd/115m per 1¾oz/50g ball) light worsted (DK) weight yarn:
    1 ball of Blood Orange shade 445 (C)

## Hooks and equipment

US size H/8 (5mm) and US size C/2–D/3 (3mm) crochet hooks

Yarn needle

## Finished measurements

Coasters: diameter 4¾in (12cm)

Basket: diameter 5¼in (13cm), height 1½in (3.5cm)

## Gauge (tension)

Rounds 1–4 of Coaster = 2in (5cm) diameter, using a US size H/8 (5mm) crochet hook and Wool and the Gang Shiny Happy Cotton.

## Abbreviations

See page 94.

## Coaster

(make 6)
Using US size H/8 (5mm) hook and A, make a magic ring.
**Round 1:** 6sc in ring, sl st in top of first sc to join. *(6 sts)*
**Round 2:** Ch1 (does not count as st throughout), [2sc in next st] 6 times, sl st in top of ch-1 to join. *(12 sts)*
**Round 3:** Ch1, [1sc in next st, 2sc in next st] 6 times, sl st in top of ch-1 to join. *(18 sts)*
**Round 4:** Ch1, 1sc in first st, 2sc in next st, [1sc in each of next 2 sts, 2sc in next st] 5 times, 1sc in last st, sl st in top of ch-1 to join. *(24 sts)*
**Round 5:** Ch1, [1sc in each of next 3 sts, 2sc in next st] 6 times, sl st in top of ch-1 to join. *(30 sts)*
**Round 6:** Ch1, 1sc in each of next 2 sts, 2sc in next st, [1sc in each of next 4 sts, 2sc in next st] 5 times, 1sc in each of next 2 sts, sl st in top of ch-1 to join. *(36 sts)*
**Round 7:** Ch1, [1sc in each of next 5 sts, 2sc in next st] 6 times, sl st in top of ch-1 to join. *(42 sts)*
**Round 8:** Ch1, 1sc in each of next 3 sts, 2sc in next st, [1sc in each of next 6 sts, 2sc in next st] 5 times, 1sc in each of next 3 sts, sl st in top of ch-1 to join. *(48 sts)*
Fasten off A.

## BORDER

Using US size C/2–D/3 (3mm) hook, with RS facing, join in C with a sl st to any st around edge of coaster.
**Round 1:** Ch1, *1sc in next st, 2sc in next st; rep from * around edge of coaster, sl st in ch-1 to join. *(72 sts)*
**Round 2:** Ch1, working in back loops only, sl st in next st, *ch1, sl st in next st; rep from * around edge of coaster, sl st in ch-1 to join.
Fasten off C.

**TIP** When working the rounds, finish each round by joining back to the beginning with a slip stitch. Chain 1 and work the first stitch from the next round in the single crochet at the base of the chain. This will give you a straight, neat join at the end of each round.

## Basket

Using US size H/8 (5mm) hook and B, make a magic ring.
**Rounds 1–8:** Work as Rounds 1–8 of coaster. *(48 sts)*
**Round 9:** Ch1, [1sc in each of next 7 sts, 2sc in next st] 6 times, sl st in top of ch-1 to join. *(54 sts)*
**Round 10:** Ch1, 1sc in each of next 4 sts, 2sc in next st, [1sc in each of next 8 sts, 2sc in next st] 5 times, 1sc in each of next 4 sts, sl st in top of ch-1 to join. *(60 sts)*
**Round 11:** Ch1, [1sc in each of next 9 sts, 2sc in next st] 6 times, sl st in top of ch-1 to join. *(66 sts)*
**Round 12:** Ch1, 1sc in each of next 5 sts, 2sc in next st, [1sc in each of next 10 sts, 2sc in next st] 5 times, 1sc in each of next 5 sts, sl st in top of ch-1 to join. *(72 sts)*
**Round 13:** Ch1, turn work so that underside of basket base is facing you, working in back loops only, 1sc in each st around, sl st in top of first st of round, do not turn.
**Round 14:** Ch1, now working in both loops again as usual, 1sc in each st around, sl st in top of ch-1 to join.
**Rounds 15–19:** Rep Round 14.
Fasten off.

## Making up and finishing

### FINISHING THE COASTER

Using US size C/2–D/3 (3mm) hook and C, with RS facing, work a round of sl st one round in from the border, inserting hook right through the coaster.
Fasten off.

### FINISHING THE BASKET

Using US size C/2–D/3 (3mm) hook, with RS facing, join C with a sl st in any st around top edge of basket, ch1, sl st in next st, *ch1, sl st in the next st, rep from * around edge of basket, sl st in top of ch-1 to join.
Fasten off.
Using US size C/2–D/3 (3mm) hook and A, with RS facing, work a round of sl st one round down from the border, inserting hook right through the side of the basket.
Fasten off.

# Hot water bottle cover

Nothing quite beats snuggling up with a hot water bottle on a cold night—and when it's tucked inside this cozy cover both you and the hot water bottle will stay toasty and warm for hours. Worked as a simple rectangle, the cover is a generous fit for all standard-sized hot water bottles.

**SKILL LEVEL** ● ● ●

## Yarn and materials

Debbie Bliss Baby Cashmerino
(55% wool, 33% acrylic, 12% cashmere,
137yd/125m per 1¾oz/50g ball)
sport (5-ply) weight yarn:
   2 balls each of:
   Flame shade 306 (A)
   Mustard shade 316 (D)
   1 ball each of:
   Camel shade 102 (B)
   White shade 100 (C)

19¾in (50cm) of ⅞in (22mm)
wide coordinating ribbon

1 hot water bottle, standard size

## Hook and equipment

US size E/4 (3.5mm) crochet hook

Yarn needle

## Finished measurements

Width 8¼in (21cm), length 15in (38cm)

## Gauge (tension)

15 sts x 15 rows = 2½ x 2⅜in (6.5 x 6cm)
working single crochet, using a US size
E/4 (3.5mm) crochet hook.

## Abbreviations

See page 94.

## Special abbreviation

**MB (make bobble):** using yarn that is laid
along top of row, [yarn over hook, insert
hook in stitch, yarn over hook, pull yarn
through work, yarn over hook, pull
yarn through first 2 loops on hook]
4 times all in same stitch, using main
color yarn over hook, pull through
all loops on hook

## Cover

Using US size E/4 (3.5mm) hook and A, ch91.

**Row 1:** 1sc in second ch from hook, 1sc in each ch to end. *(90 sts).*

Turn at end of this row and every foll row. Do not fasten off a yarn until instructed to do so, instead carry it loosely up the side between rows. Unless otherwise indicated, the color used for the first ch1 of each row should be used for the remainder of the row; join new colors when necessary.

**Rows 2-4:** Ch1 (does not count as st throughout), 1sc in each st to end.

**Rows 5 and 6:** Ch1 in D, 1sc in each st to end.

**Row 7:** Ch1 in A, 1sc in each st to end, fasten off A.

**Row 8:** Ch1 in B, 1sc in each st to end.

**Row 9:** Ch1 in B, lay D along top of row, 1sc in B in each of next sts, MB in D, *1sc in B in each of next 8 sts, MB in D; rep from * to last 4 sts, 1sc in B in each of last 4 sts.

**Row 10:** Ch1 in B, 1sc in each st to end, fasten off B.

**Row 11:** Ch1 in A, 1sc in each st to end, fasten off A.

**Rows 12 and 13:** Ch1 in D, 1sc in each st to end.

**Row 14:** Ch1 in C, lay B along top of row, *1sc in C in each of next 2 sts working yoh of last st in B, 1sc in B in each of next 2 sts working yoh of last st in C; rep from * to last 2 sts, 1sc in C in each of last 2 sts working yoh of last st in B.

**Row 15:** Ch1 in B, lay C along top of row, *1sc in B in each of next 2 sts working yoh of last st in C, 1sc in C in each of next 2 sts working yoh of last st in B; rep from * to last 2 sts, 1sc in B in each of last 2 sts, fasten off B and C.

**Rows 16-18:** Ch1 in A, 1sc in each st to end.

**Row 19:** Ch1 in D, 1sc in each st to end, fasten off D.

**Row 20:** Ch1 in B, 1sc in each st to end.

**Row 21:** Ch1 in B, lay A along top of row, 1sc in B in each of next 4 sts, MB in A, *1sc in B in each of next 8 sts, MB in A; rep from * to last 4 sts, 1sc in B in each of last 4 sts.

**Row 22:** Ch1 in B, 1sc in each st to end, fasten off B.

**Row 23:** Ch1 in D, 1sc in each st to end, fasten off D.

**Rows 24 and 25:** Ch1 in A, 1sc in each st to end, fasten off A.

**Rows 26 and 27:** Rep Rows 14 and 15.

**Rows 28-30:** Ch1 in D, 1sc in each st to end.

**Row 31:** Ch1 in A, 1sc in each st to end, fasten off A.

**Row 32:** Ch1 in B, 1sc in each st to end.

**Row 33:** Ch1 in B, lay D along top of row, 1sc in B in each of next 4 sts, MB in D, *1sc in B in each of next 8 sts, MB in D; rep from * to last 4 sts, 1sc in B in each of last 4 sts.

**Row 34:** Ch1 in B, 1sc in each st to end, fasten off B.

**Row 35:** Ch1 in A, 1sc in each st to end, fasten off A.

**Rows 36 and 37:** Ch1 in D, 1sc in each st to end, fasten off D.

**Rows 38-61:** Rep Rows 14-37.

**Rows 62-83:** Rep Rows 14-35.

**Rows 84 and 85:** Ch1 in D, 1sc in each st to end.

**Row 86 (eyelet row):** Ch1 in D, 1sc in each of next 5 sts, *ch3, miss next 3 sts, 1sc in each of next 4 sts; rep from * to last 8 sts, ch3, miss next 3 sts, 1sc in each of last 5 sts.

**Rows 87-88:** Ch1 in D, 1sc in each st to end.

**Row 89:** Join in C, ch1, lay B along top of row, *1sc in C in each of next 2 sts working yoh of last st in B, 1sc in B in each of next 2 sts working yoh of last st in C; rep from * to last 2 sts, 1sc in C in each of last 2 sts working yoh of last st in B.

**Row 90:** Ch1 in B, lay C along top of row, *1sc in B in each of next 2 sts working yoh of last st in C, 1sc in C in each of next 2 sts working yoh of last st in B; rep from * to last 2 sts, 1sc in B in each of last 2 sts, fasten off B and C.

**Rows 91-94:** Ch1 in A, 1sc in each st to end.

**Row 95:** Ch1 in D, 1sc in each st to end, fasten off D.

**Row 96:** Ch1 in B, 1sc in each st to end.

**Row 97:** Ch1 in B, lay A along top of row, 1sc in B in each of next 4 sts, MB in A, *1sc in B in each of next 8 sts, MB in A; rep from * to last 4 sts, 1sc in B in each of last 4 sts.

**Row 98:** Ch1 in B, 1sc in each st to end.

**Row 99:** Ch1 in D, 1sc in each st to end.

**Rows 100 and 101:** Ch1 in A, 1sc in each st to end, fasten off A.

**Rows 102 and 103:** Rep Rows 14 and 15.

**Row 104:** Ch1 in D, 1sc in each st to end.

Fasten off.

## Making up and finishing

### EDGING

With the RS of the work facing, using a US size E/4 (3.5mm) hook, join D in the top left-hand corner of the cover.

**Row 1 (RS):** Work 1sc in each row end down left-hand edge, turn.

**Row 1 (WS):** Ch1, 1sc in each st to end.

Fasten off.

Rep for the right-hand edge of the cover.

Sew in or knot together all ends on the inside of the cover. With WS together and using D, join the two side edges together with a sc seam—this seam will be a feature on the center back of the cover. Center the sc seam on one side, turn the cover WS out and sew the bottom edge closed. Turn RS out again.

Place the hot water bottle inside. Thread coordinating ribbon through the eyelets (Row 86), with the two ends meeting center front, and tie the ends in a bow.

# Waffle stitch placemats

Crocheted in waffle stitch, these placemats work up to give a lovely, thick, textured protector to use on your dining table. Edged in crab stitch in a contrast color they can be personalized to match your plates. The yarn used in this pattern is 100% cotton and fully washable.

## SKILL LEVEL ● ●

### Yarn and materials

*For one placemat:*

Cascade Yarns Ultra Pima (100% cotton, 219yd/200m per 3½oz/100g ball) light worsted (DK) weight yarn:
   1 ball of Sage shade 3720 (A)

Cascade Yarns Noble Cotton (100% cotton, 220yd/201m per 3½oz/100g ball) light worsted (DK) weight yarn:
   Small amount of Pale Gold shade 15 (B)

### Hooks and equipment

US size E/4 (3.5mm) and US size C/2–D/3 (3mm) crochet hooks

Yarn needle

### Finished measurements

Width 12¼in (31cm), length 8¾in (22cm)

### Gauge (tension)

14 sts x 6 rows = 2⅜ x 2in (6 x 5cm) working waffle stitch, using a US size E/4 (3.5mm) crochet hook and Cascade Ultra Pima.

15 sts x 15 rows = 2½ x 2¾in (6.5 x 7cm) working single crochet using a US size C/2–D/3 (3mm) crochet hook and Cascade Yarns Noble Cotton.

### Abbreviations

See page 94.

### Special abbreviation

**FPdc (front post double crochet):** yarn over hook, from front of work insert hook from right to left behind post of next st on prev round and through to front again, yarn over hook and pull loop through, [yarn over hook, draw through 2 loops] twice

## Placemat

Using US size E/4 (3.5mm) hook and A, ch70.
**Row 1 (WS):** 1dc in third ch from hook, 1dc in each ch to end, turn. *(68 sts)*
**Row 2:** Ch1 (does not count as st throughout), 1dc in each of first 2 sts, *1FPdc in next st, 1dc in each of next 2 sts; rep from * to end, turn.

~~~~~~~~~~~~~~~~~~~~~~~~~~~~~

**TIP** Working one chain, rather than two, at the start of each row keeps the edges straight and neat.

**Row 3:** Ch1, 1dc in first st, 1FPdc in next st, 1dc in next st, *1FPdc in each of next 2 sts, 1dc in next st; rep from * to last 2 sts, 1FPdc in next st, 1dc in last st, turn.
Rep Rows 2 and 3 thirteen times.
Rep Row 2 once more.
Fasten off.

### BORDER

**Round 1:** With RS facing join in A in bottom right-hand corner, 1sc in each row end up right-hand side, 2sc in corner st, 1sc in each st across top edge, 2sc in corner st, 1sc in each row end down to bottom left-hand corner, 1sc in each st across bottom edge, 2sc in corner st, sl st in top of first sc to join.

**Round 2:** Ch1, work crab st around mat as follows: working clockwise with RS facing, [inserting hook from back to front, work 1sc in next st to right] to end of round, sl st in top of ch-1 to join.
Fasten off.

### Making up and finishing

Using US size C/2–D/3 (3mm) hook and B, work 2 rounds of sl st working from the top of the placemat through to the bottom, the first round being just under the crab st and the second round being on the inside of first border round.
Fasten off and sew in any ends (see page 87).

# Christmas place settings

For something a little different, why not make all of your Christmas dinner guests a mini festive wreath? They are very quick to complete and can be personalized with individual name tags.

## SKILL LEVEL ●

### Yarn and materials

*For eight mini wreaths:*
DMC Natura XL (100% cotton, 82yd/75m per 3½oz/100g ball) super bulky (super chunky) weight yarn:
 1 ball of shade 85 (A)

Cascade Yarns Ultra Pima Fine (100% cotton, 137yd/125m per 1¾oz/50g ball) sport (5-ply) weight yarn:
 1 ball each of:
 Sprout shade 3740 (B)
 Wine shade 3713 (C)

8 wooden rings, 2¾in (70mm) diameter

8 gold craft jingle bells, ⅞in (20mm) size

8 small card stock name tags

Approx. 1yd (1m) of ⅜in (10mm) wide red gingham ribbon

### Hooks and equipment

US size J/10 (6mm) and US size 0 (2mm) crochet hooks

Yarn needle

Hot glue gun

### Finished measurements

3¼in (8cm) diameter

### Gauge (tension)

5 sts x 5 rows = 1½ x 2in (4 x 5cm) working single crochet, using a US size J/10 (6mm) crochet hook and DMC Natura XL.

15 sts x 15 rows = 2¼ x 2⅜in (5.5 x 6cm) working single crochet, using a US size 0 (2mm) crochet hook and Cascade Yarns Ultra Pima Fine.

### Abbreviations

See page 94.

### Special abbreviation

**MP (make picot):** ch2, sl st in second ch from hook

## Wreath

(make 8)
Attach A to the wooden ring with a knot.
Using US size J/10 (6mm) hook, work sc all around the ring, sl st in top of first sc to join.
Fasten off, leaving a long yarn tail.

## Holly leaf

(make 16)
Using US size 0 (2mm) hook and B, ch6.
Sl st in second ch from hook, [MP, sl st in next st] 3 times, sl st in next st, MP (tip made), working down opposite side of ch, sl st in next st, [MP, sl st in next st] twice, sl st in next st.
Fasten off.

## Making up and finishing

Using a yarn needle threaded with C, work two or three French knots (see page 90) at the base of each leaf for the berries.
Thread a bell onto the long yarn tail left at the end of the wreath, and then sew in the yarn tail to secure at the back of the wreath.
Fasten off.
Use a hot glue gun to stick two holly leaves at the base of each wreath. Make small bows in gingham ribbon and glue at the top of each wreath. Tie on a name tag.

# CHAPTER 2
# Blankets & Pillows

# Simple checkered blanket

If you love a little bit of extra warmth on those chilly evenings, but a full blanket is a little too much, this lap-sized blanket will perfectly fit the bill. Worked in simple rows of single crochet, this pattern allows you to crochet a very complicated-looking blanket with absolute ease. The two colors are worked by laying one color along the top of each row you are working on so that the two colors can be alternated easily throughout the row.

## SKILL LEVEL ● ●

### Yarn and materials
Cascade Yarns 220 Superwash (100% superwash wool, 220yd/200m per 3½oz/100g ball) light worsted (DK) weight yarn:
    4 balls in each of:
    Seagrass shade 350 (A)
    Winter White shade 910A (B)

### Hooks and equipment
US size 7 (4.5mm) and US size G/6 (4mm) crochet hooks

Yarn needle

4 stitch markers

### Finished measurements
30¼in (77cm) wide x 32in (81cm) long

### Gauge (tension)
20 sts x 22 rows = 4in (10cm) square working single crochet, using a US size 7 (4.5mm) crochet hook.

### Abbreviations
See page 94.

## Blanket
Using US size 7 (4.5mm) hook and A, ch161 loosely.
**Note:** After working each 9th sc always gently pull on the color lying along the top of the row to make sure it is lying taut under the stitches.
**Row 1:** Lay B along top of chain, beg in second ch from hook, *using A, 1sc in each of next 10 sc, working yoh of last st in B, lay A along top of chain, using B, 1sc in each of next 10 sc, working yoh of last st in A; rep from * to last 20 ch, using A, 1sc in each of next 10 sc, working yoh of last st in B, using B, 1sc in each of last 10 sc, turn. *(16 10-sc squares in alt colors)*
Ch1 in B, catching in A, so both yarns are carried up neatly to next row.
Lay color not in use along top of row throughout.

**Row 2:** *Using B, 1sc in each of next 10 sc, working yoh of last st in A, using A, 1sc in each of next 10 sc, working yoh of last st in B; rep from * to last 20 sts, using B, 1sc in each of next 10 sc, working yoh of last st in A, using A, 1sc in each of last 10 sc, turn.
Ch1 in A, catching in B, so both yarns are carried up neatly to next row.
**Row 3:** *Using A, 1sc in each of next 10 sc, working yoh of last st in B, using B, 1sc in each of next 10 sc, working yoh of last st in A; rep from * to last 20 sts, using A, 1sc in each of next 10 sc, working yoh of last st in B, using B, 1sc in each of last 10 sc, turn.
Ch1 in B, catching in A, so both yarns are carried up neatly to next row.
**Rows 4–11:** Rep Rows 2 and 3, at end of each row working ch1 and catching in second color so both yarns are carried up to next row. Work final yoh of Row 11 in A.
Ch1 in B, catching in A, so both yarns are carried up neatly to next row.

**Row 12:** *Using A, 1sc in each of next 10 sc, working yoh of last st in B, using B, 1sc in each of next 10 sc, working yoh of last st in A; rep from * to last 20 sts, using A, 1sc in each of next 10 sc, working yoh of last st in B, using B, 1sc in each of last 10 sc, turn. *(16 10-sc squares in alt colors)*

**Row 13:** *Using B, 1sc in each of next 10 sc, working yoh of last st in A, using A, 1sc in each of next 10 sc, working yoh of last st in B; rep from * to last 20 sts, using B, 1sc in each of next 10 sc, working yoh of last st in A, using A, 1sc in each of last 10 sc, turn.

Ch1 in A, catching in B, so both yarns are carried up neatly to next row.

**Rows 14–21:** Rep Rows 12 and 13, at end of each row working ch-1 and catching in second color so both yarns are carried up to next row.

**Row 22:** Rep Row 12, working final yoh in A.

At end of Row 22 you will completed 32 alt squares in check pattern.

Cont working in pattern, until you have worked a total of 16 rows of squares from bottom of blanket to top. Fasten off.

## BORDER

**Round 1:** Using US size G/6 (4mm) hook and with RS facing, join in A at bottom right-hand corner with a sl st, 1sc in same st, working along right-hand side, *miss next row end, 2sc in next row end; rep from * to top right-hand corner, 3sc in corner st, PM in center st of 3-sc, 1sc in each st along top, 3sc in corner st, PM in center st of 3-sc, working along left-hand side, *miss next row end, 2sc in next row end; rep from * to bottom left-hand corner, 3sc in corner st, PM in center st of 3-sc, 1sc in each st along bottom edge, 2sc in corner st, PM in second st of 2-sc, sl st in first st to join.

**Round 2:** Ch1 (does not count as st throughout), 1sc in each st around, working 3sc in marked st at corners and moving marker to center st of each corner, sl st in first st to join.

Fasten off A.

**Round 3:** Join in B at bottom right-hand corner with sl st, 1sc BLO in same st, 1sc BLO in each st around, working 3sc BLO in marked st at corners and moving marker to center st of each corner, sl st in first st to join.

**Round 4:** Ch1, 1sc in each st around, working 3sc in marked st at corners and moving marker to center st of each corner, sl st in first st to join.

Fasten off B.

**Round 5:** Join in A at bottom right-hand corner with sl st, 1sc BLO in same st, *ch2, 1sc BLO in second ch from hook, sl st BLO in each of next 2 sts, 1sc BLO in next st; rep from * to end (you may not end with a complete rep), sl st in first st to join.

Fasten off.

## Making up and finishing

Sew in all ends (see page 87).

# Patchwork pillow

This pillow is all about texture and, whether worked in bright colors or coordinating neutrals, it will make a beautiful addition to any cozy corner in your home. Made up of bobbly and striped patchwork squares on the front, with back panels worked in seed (moss) stitch, it will give you the chance to try out lots of textured crochet while working with just single crochet and double crochet stitches. The cover has a simple overlap opening on the back, and a small ruffle edging to finish it off.

**SKILL LEVEL** ● ● ●

### Yarn and materials
Cascade Yarns 220 Superwash
(100% superwash wool, 220yd/200m
per 3½oz/100g ball) light worsted (DK)
weight yarn:
    4 balls of Ash Rose shade 229 (A)
    1 ball of Frosted Almond shade 228 (B)

17 x 17in (43 x 43cm) pillow form

### Hook and equipment
US size E/4 (3.5mm) crochet hook

Yarn needle

Pins

### Finished measurements
17 x 17in (43 x 43cm)

### Gauge (tension)
24 sts x 28 rows = 4in (10cm) square
working single crochet, using a
US size E/4 (3.5mm) crochet hook.

### Abbreviations
See page 94.

### Special abbreviation
**MB (make bobble):** using yarn laid along top of row, [yoh, insert hook in st and pull yarn through, yoh, pull yarn through first 2 loops on hook] 3 times all in same st, using main color, yoh, pull through all loops on hook

## Bobbly square

(make 8)
Using A, ch20.
**Row 1:** 1sc in second ch from hook and in each ch to end, turn. *(19 sts)*
**Row 2:** Ch1 (does not count as st throughout), 1sc in each st to end, turn.
**Row 3 (bobble row 1):** Ch1, lay B along top of last row, 1sc in A in each of first 3 sts, pull up B and MB in next st, *1sc in A in each of next 3 sts, MB in B in next st; rep from * twice more to make 4 bobbles in total, 1sc in A in each of last 3 sts, fasten off B, turn.
**Rows 4–6:** Ch1, 1sc in each st to end, turn.
**Row 7 (bobble row 2):** Ch1, lay B along top of last row, 1sc in A in first st, pull up B and MB in next st, *1sc in A in each of next 3 sts, MB in B in next st; rep from * 3 more times to make 5 bobbles in total, 1sc in A in last st, fasten off B, turn.

**Rows 8–10:** Ch1, 1sc in each st to end, turn.
**Row 11 (bobble row 1):** Rep Row 3.
**Rows 12–14:** Ch1, 1sc in each st to end, turn.
**Row 15 (bobble row 2):** Rep Row 7.
**Rows 16–18:** Ch1, 1sc in each st to end, turn.
**Row 19 (bobble row 1):** Rep Row 3.
**Rows 20–22:** Ch1, 1sc in each st to end, turn.
Fasten off and sew in ends (see page 87).

### EDGING
**Round 1:** With RS of square facing, join in A at top left-hand corner, 1sc in each row edge down left-hand side, ch1, 1sc in each st along bottom edge, ch1, 1sc in each row end up right-hand side, ch1, sl st in beg of top edge.
Fasten off and sew in ends.

## Striped square

(make 8)

Using A, ch20.

**Row 1:** 1sc in second ch from hook and in each ch to end, turn. *(19 sts)*

Do not fasten off A. Join in B.

**Row 2:** Using B, ch1 (does not count as st throughout), 1sc in each st to end, turn.

**Row 3:** Ch1, 1sc in each st to end, turn.

Do not fasten off B.

**Row 4:** Using A, ch1, 1sc in each st to end, turn.

**Row 5:** Ch1, 1 sc in each st to end, turn.

**Rows 6 and 7:** Rep Rows 2 and 3.

**Rows 8 and 9:** Rep Rows 4 and 5.

**Rows 10 and 11:** Rep Rows 2 and 3.

**Rows 12 and 13:** Rep Rows 4 and 5.

**Rows 14 and 15:** Rep Rows 2 and 3.

**Rows 16 and 17:** Rep Rows 4 and 5.

**Rows 18 and 19:** Rep Rows 2 and 3.

**Rows 20 and 21:** Rep Rows 4 and 5.

Fasten off A.

**Rows 22 and 23:** Rep Rows 2 and 3.

Fasten off B.

**Row 24:** Rep Row 4, do not turn.

### EDGING

**Round 1:** Ch1, 1sc in each row edge down left-hand side, ch1, 1sc in each st along bottom edge, ch1, 1sc in each row end up right-hand side, ch1, sl st in beg of top edge.

Fasten off and sew in ends.

### JOINING THE SQUARES

Lay squares on a flat surface, in correct pattern.

For vertical seams, place bottom left square and square to right with WS tog, join in A at bottom right, 1sc in each row end through both layers to join squares.

At top of first two squares place next two squares WS tog and cont vertical seam as before. Rep twice more so first two vertical rows of eight squares are joined.

Open out joined rows to add third vertical row of squares in same way, rep to add fourth row.

All 16 squares now joined with three vertical seams.

For horizontal seams, fold two strips horizontally, WS tog, join in A, 1sc in each st through both layers to join rows. Rep twice more to join rem strips.

All four rows now joined with three horizontal seams.

### EDGING

With RS facing, join in A at bottom right-hand corner with a sl st, 1sc in same st, 1sc in each row end up right-hand side to last st, 1sc in last st, ch2, 1sc in each st along top to last st, 1sc in last st, ch2, 1sc in each row end down left-hand side to last st, 1sc in last st, ch2, 1sc in each st along bottom edge to last st, 1sc in last st, ch2, sl st in first st.

Fasten off and sew in ends.

## Upper and lower back panels

(make 2)

Using A, ch79.

**Row 1:** 1sc in second ch from hook, *1dc in next ch, 1sc in next ch; rep from * to last ch, 1dc in last ch, turn. *(78 sts)*

**Row 2:** Ch1 (does not count as st throughout), 1sc in first st, *1dc in next st, 1sc in next st; rep from * to last st, 1dc in last st, turn.

Rep Row 2 until piece measures 9in (23cm). Do not fasten off.

### EDGING

Ch1, 1sc in each row end down left-hand side, ch1, 1sc in each st along bottom edge, ch1, 1sc in each row end up right-hand side, ch1, 1 sc in each st along top edge, sl st in top of left-hand edge.

Fasten off and sew in ends.

## Making up and finishing

Lay the front panel on a flat surface, RS down. Place one of the back pieces at the bottom of the front panel, RS up. Place the other back piece at the top of the front panel, RS up, so that it overlaps the lower back panel. Pin all pieces together around the four sides of the pillow.

### EDGING

Turn the cover over, with RS of front facing.

**Round 1:** Join in A at bottom right-hand corner with a sl st, 1sc in same st through all layers, *1sc through all layers along edge to corner, 3sc through all layers in corner st; rep from * to end, sl st in first st to join.

**Round 2:** Ch1, *3sc in next st, 4sc in next st; rep from * to end, sl st in first st to join.

Fasten off and sew in ends. Insert pillow form.

# Flower baby blanket

There can be nothing more special than spending time making a baby blanket—and this simple but modern design makes the perfect, unique gift for any new arrival. Worked in 100% cotton yarn it is light yet warm, and fully washable. The blanket is worked in single crochet and the daisies are made separately and sewn on afterward.

## SKILL LEVEL ●

### Yarn and materials
Cascade Yarns Ultra Pima (100% cotton, 219yd/200m per 3½oz/100g ball) light worsted (DK) weight yarn:
  4 balls of Veiled Rose shade
    3840 (A)
  1 ball in each of:
  Yellow Rose shade 3743 (B)
  White shade 3728 (C)

### Hooks and equipment
US size G/6 (4mm) and US size E/4 (3.5mm) crochet hooks

Yarn needle

Safety pins

Sewing needle and thread

### Finished measurements
Width 22½in (57cm), length 27½in (70cm)

One flower measures approx. 2⅜in (6cm) diameter

### Gauge (tension)
15 sts x 15 rows = 3 x 2½in (7.5 x 6.5cm) working single crochet, using a US size G/6 (4mm) crochet hook.

### Abbreviations
See page 94.

## Blanket
Using US size G/6 (4mm) hook and A, ch113.
**Row 1:** 1sc in second ch from hook, 1sc in each ch to end, turn. *(112 sts)*
**Row 2:** Ch1 (does not count as st throughout), 1sc in each st to end, turn.
Rep Row 2 until work measures 25½in (64.5cm), ending with RS facing. Do not turn and do not fasten off A at end of last row.

### BORDER
**Round 1:** Work a second sc in final st of prev row, then work 1sc in each row end down left-hand side, 2sc in corner st, 1sc in each st along bottom edge, 2sc in corner st, 1sc in each row end up right-hand side, sl st in top of first sc of prev row to join.
Fasten off A.
**Round 2:** With RS facing, join C at top right-hand corner of blanket, ch1, [1sc in each st to corner, 2sc in corner st] 4 times, sl st in top of ch-1 to join.
**Round 3:** *Ch2, sl st in each of next 2 sts; rep from * around edge of blanket. Finish off.

## Daisy
(make 13)
Using US size E/4 (3.5mm) hook and B, make a magic ring.
**Round 1:** 7sc into ring, sl st in top of first sc to join round. *(7 sts)*
**Round 2:** Ch1 (does not count as st), 2sc in each st to end, sl st in top of first sc to join round. *(14 sts)*
Fasten off B.
**Round 3:** Join C in any sc of central ring, *ch6, working back down ch, miss first ch, 1hdc in each of next 5 ch, sl st in each of next 2 sts on central ring; rep from * 6 times to make 7 petals in total, sl st in base of first petal to join round.
Fasten off.

## Making up and finishing
Sew in any ends (see page 87). Lay the blanket RS up on a flat surface, and position the daisies where you want them to be. Pin the flowers in place with safety pins. Using a sewing needle and thread stitch the daisies securely onto the blanket.

# Spotted pompom pillow

With spots and pompoms galore, this pillow will add a wonderful contemporary touch to any home. The cover has a simple overlap opening at the back so that it can be removed for washing.

**SKILL LEVEL** ●

### Yarn and materials
Cascade Yarns Ultra Pima (100% cotton, 219yd/200m per 3½oz/100g ball) light worsted (DK) weight yarn:
    4 balls of Natural shade 3718 (A)

Scheepjes Sweetheart Soft (100% polyester, 167yd/153m per 3½oz/100g ball) bulky (chunky) weight yarn:
    1 ball of Lilac shade 13 (B)

2¼yd (2m) gray pompom edging

16 x 16in (40 x 40cm) pillow form

3 snap fasteners

3 decorative buttons

### Hooks and equipment
US size G/6 (4mm) and US size C/2-D/3 (3mm) crochet hooks

Yarn needle

Safety pins

Sewing needle and thread

### Finished measurements
18¼ x 18¼in (46 x 46cm)

### Gauge (tension)
15 sts x 15 rows = 3 x 2¾in (7.5 x 7cm) working single crochet, using a US size G/6 (4mm) crochet hook and Cascade Yarns Ultra Pima.

### Abbreviations
See page 94.

## Pillow cover front panel
Using US size G/6 (4mm) hook and A, ch81.
**Row 1:** 1sc in second ch from hook, 1sc in each ch to end, turn. *(80 sts)*
**Row 2:** Ch1 (does not count as st throughout), 1sc in each st to end, turn.
Rep Row 2 until work measures 15½in (39.5cm), ending with RS facing, do not turn.

### EDGING
**Round 1:** Work a second sc in final st of prev row, then work 1sc in each row end down left-hand side, 2sc in corner st, 1sc in each st along bottom edge, 2sc in corner st, 1sc in each row end up right-hand side, 1sc in same st as first sc of prev row, sl st in top of first sc of prev row to join round. Fasten off.
**Round 2:** With RS facing, join B at top right-hand corner of panel, ch1, [1sc in each st to corner, 2sc in corner st] 4 times, sl st in top of ch-1 to join round. Fasten off.

## Upper back panel
Using US size G/6 (4mm) hook and A, ch81.
**Row 1:** 1sc in second ch from hook, 1sc in each ch to end, turn. *(80 sts)*
**Row 2:** Ch1 (does not count as st), 1sc in each st to end, turn.
Rep Row 2 until work measures 8¼in (21cm), ending with RS facing, do not turn.

### EDGING
**Round 1:** Work a second sc in final st of prev row, then work 1sc in each row end down left-hand side, 2sc in corner st, 1sc in each st along bottom edge, 2sc in corner st, 1sc in each row end up right-hand side, 1sc in same st as first sc of prev row, sl st in top of first sc of prev row to join round. Fasten off.

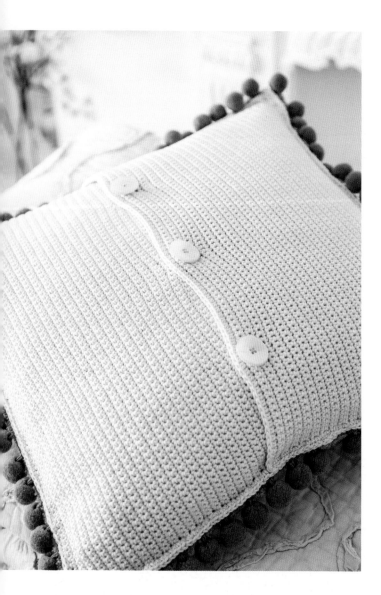

## Lower back panel

Using US size G/6 (4mm) hook and A, ch81.

**Row 1:** 1sc in second ch from hook, 1sc in each ch to end, turn. *(80 sts)*

**Row 2:** Ch1 (does not count as st), 1sc in each st to end, turn.

Rep Row 2 until work measures 9½in (24cm), ending with RS facing, do not turn.

### EDGING

**Round 1:** Work a second sc in final st of prev row, then work 1sc in each row end down left-hand side, 2sc in corner st, 1sc in each st along bottom edge, 2sc in corner st, 1sc in each row end up right-hand side, 1sc in same st as first sc of prev row, sl st in top of first sc of prev row to join round. Fasten off.

## Spots

(make 19)

Work in a continuous spiral.

Using US size C/2–D/3 (3mm) hook and B, make a magic ring.

**Round 1:** 8sc into ring. *(8 sts)*

**Round 2:** 2sc in each st to end, sl st in top of first sc to join round. *(16 sts)*

Fasten off.

## Making up and finishing

Place the front cover RS down with the pompom edging around all four sides, making sure the pompoms hang over the edge. Add two back panels WS down on top, with outer edges aligned so they overlap in the center. Pin all the layers in place with safety pins. Using a sewing needle and thread, stitch the sides together all the way around the pillow, making sure the pompom edging is stitched in too. Put the pillow form into the cover and pin across the join at the back to hold the cover in place while you position and attach the spots to the front of the pillow. Turn the pillow over so that front is facing you and position the spots where you want them to be. Hold them in place with safety pins, then slide the pillow form out. Using a sewing needle and thread, stitch the spots securely in place being careful not to stitch right through to the back layers of the cover.

Place the pillow form back inside and stitch the three snap fasteners evenly spaced along the inside of the overlap to close the cover. Using a sewing needle and thread, sew the three buttons onto the back of the pillow, directly above the snap fasteners.

**TIP** To prevent you accidentally sewing the front of the pillow to the back when sewing on the spots, slide a piece of card stock inside the cover.

# Textured pillow with pompoms

This rectangular pillow is worked in alpine stitch, to match the textured lap blanket on page 52. The pillow is finished with a pompom at each corner as a fun touch and to keep it coordinating with the blanket.

**SKILL LEVEL** ● ●

### Yarn and materials
Lion Brand Wool Ease (80% acrylic, 20% wool, 197yd/180m per 3oz/85g ball) worsted (aran) weight yarn:
  3 balls of Natural Heather shade 098 (A)
  1 ball of Fisherman shade 099 (B)
16 x 12in (40 x 30cm) pillow form
3 snap fasteners
3 buttons

### Hook and equipment
US size I/9 (5.5mm) crochet hook
Yarn needle
1½in (35mm) pompom maker

### Finished measurements
Width 16in (40cm), height 12in (30cm)

### Gauge (tension)
15 sts x 15 rows = 4¼ x 4in (10.5 x 10cm) working Rows 1–3 and then Rows 4–7 three times, using a US size I/9 (5.5mm) crochet hook.

### Abbreviations
See page 94.

### Special abbreviation
**FPdc (front post double crochet):** yarn over hook, from front of work insert hook from right to left behind post of next st on prev round and through to front again, yarn over hook and pull loop through, [yarn over hook, draw through 2 loops] twice

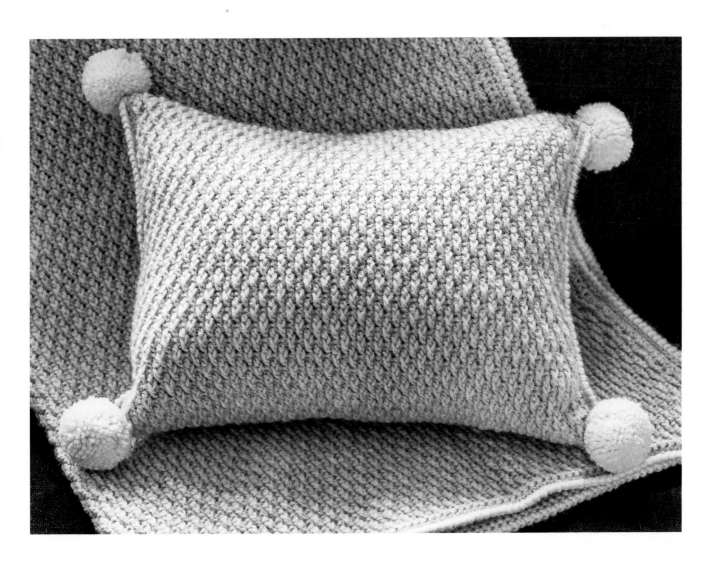

## Pillow cover

Using US size I/9 (5.5mm) hook and A, ch60.

**Row 1 (WS):** 1sc in second ch from hook, 1sc in each ch to end, turn. *(59 sts)*

**Row 2 (RS):** Ch2 (does not count as st throughout), 1dc in each st to end, turn.

**Row 3:** Ch1 (does not count as st throughout), 1sc in each st to end, turn.

**Row 4:** Ch2, *1FPdc in next st, 1dc in next st; rep from * to last st, 1dc in last st, turn.

**Row 5:** Ch1, 1sc in each st to end, turn.

**Row 6:** Ch2, 1dc in first st, *1FPdc in next st, 1dc in next st; rep from * to end, turn.

**Row 7:** Ch1, 1sc in each st to end, turn.

Rep Rows 4–7 until work measures 26in (66cm), ending on a sc row, turn.

**Final row:** Ch1, 1sc in each st to end, do not turn.

### BORDER

**Round 1:** Work a second sc in last st of prev row (corner made), work 1sc in each row end down left-hand side, 2sc in corner st, work 1sc in each st along bottom edge, 2sc in corner st, work 1sc in each row end up right-hand side of pillow, 2sc in corner st, sl st in top of first st of last row of pillow to join.

Fasten off.

**Round 2:** Join B in top right corner, *2sc in corner st, 1sc in each st to corner; rep from * 3 times, sl st in top of first sc to join.

Fasten off.

## Making up and finishing

Lay the pillow cover on a flat surface, RS down. Place the pillow form in the middle, fold the bottom of the cover up and the top of the cover down so that the pillow form is enclosed, and the two edges overlap. Pin across the join at the back of the pillow where the opening will be. Pin the sides.

### JOIN SIDES

**Row 1 (RS):** Using US size I/9 (5.5mm) hook, with RS of pillow facing and using B, work a sc seam to join layers down one side, do not fasten off, do not turn.

**Row 2:** Ch1, work crab st clockwise with RS facing as foll: [inserting hook from back to front, work 1sc in next st to the right] up side of pillow.

Fasten off.

Rep on other side of pillow.

Sew in any ends (see page 87).

Using pompom maker and B, make 4 pompoms.

Stitch one pompom securely to each corner.

Stitch the three snap fasteners into place so that the opening of the pillow is closed, and the fasteners are hidden underneath the overlapping flap. Using a sewing needle and thread, sew the three buttons onto the back of the pillow, directly above where the fasteners are.

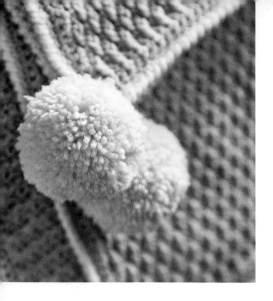

# Textured lap blanket

This beautifully soft blanket is worked in alpine stitch, which creates a wonderful texture while still giving lots of drape. It's perfect for laying over your knees on a chilly evening to add a little warmth—but without the bulk and heaviness of a larger blanket. See page 49 for the matching pillow.

## SKILL LEVEL ●●

### Yarn and materials
Lion Brand Wool Ease (80% acrylic, 20% wool, 197yd/180m per 3oz/85g ball) worsted (aran) weight yarn:
- 10 balls of Natural Heather shade 098 (A)
- 1 ball of Fisherman shade 099 (B)

### Hook and equipment
US size I/9 (5.5mm) crochet hook

Yarn needle

2½in (68mm) pompom maker

### Finished measurements
40in (102cm) square

### Gauge (tension)
15 sts x 15 rows = 4¼ x 4in (10.5 x 10cm) working Rows 1–3 and then Rows 4–7 three times, using a US size I/9 (5.5mm) crochet hook.

### Abbreviations
See page 94.

### Special abbreviation
**FPdc (front post double crochet):** yarn over hook, from front of work insert hook from right to left behind post of next st on prev round and through to front again, yarn over hook and pull loop through, [yarn over hook, draw through 2 loops] twice

## Blanket
Using US size I/9 (5.5mm) hook and A, ch152.
**Row 1 (WS):** 1sc in second ch from hook, 1sc in each ch to end, turn. *(151 sts)*
**Row 2 (RS):** Ch2 (does not countas st throughout), 1dc in each st to end, turn.
**Row 3:** Ch1 (does not count as st throughout), 1sc in each st to end, turn.
**Row 4:** Ch2, *1FPdc in next st, 1dc in next st; rep from * to last st, 1dc in last st, turn.
**Row 5:** Ch1, 1sc in each st to end, turn.
**Row 6:** Ch2, 1dc in first st, *1FPdc in next st, 1dc in next st; rep from * to end, turn.
**Row 7:** Ch1, 1sc in each st to end, turn.
Rep Rows 4–7 until work measures 37½in (95cm), ending on a sc row.
**Final row:** Ch1, 1sc in each st to end.
Fasten off.

## SIDE BORDER
Using US size I/9 (5.5mm) hook and with RS facing, join yarn A at top corner of one side edge.
**Row 1:** 1sc in each row end down side edge, turn.
**Row 2:** Ch1, 1sc in each st to end.
Fasten off.
Rep for second side.

## EDGING
Using US size I/9 (5.5mm) hook and with RS facing, join B at top right-hand corner.
**Round 1:** *2sc in first st (corner made), 1sc in each st to corner; rep from * 3 times, sl st in top of first sc to join.
**Round 2:** Ch1, work crab st clockwise with RS facing as foll: [inserting hook from back to front, work 1sc in next st to the right] to end of round, sl st in top of first st to join.
Fasten off.

## Making up and finishing
Sew in ends (see page 87).
Using pompom maker and B, make 4 pompoms.
Stitch one pompom securely to each corner.

# Bobbly rectangular pillow

With the sharp contrast of the white dots against the mustard background, this pillow will add an instant splash of sunshine brightness to any couch or armchair. The ruffle edging finishes off the sides nicely.

## SKILL LEVEL ● ●

### Yarn and materials
Cascade Yarns Spuntaneous Worsted (100% wool, 208yd/190m per 3½oz/100g ball) worsted (aran) weight yarn:
   3 balls of Gold shade 07 (A)

Debbie Bliss Baby Cashmerino (55% wool, 33% acrylic, 12% cashmere, 137yd/125m per 1¾oz/50g ball) sport (5-ply) weight yarn:
   1 ball of White shade 100 (B)

16½ x 12in (42 x 30cm) pillow form

3 snap fasteners

3 buttons

### Hook and equipment
US size 7 (4.5mm) crochet hook

Pins

Sewing needle and thread

### Finished measurements
Width 16½in (42cm), height 12in (30cm)

### Gauge (tension)
15 sts x 15 rows = 3¼ x 3in (8.5 x 7.5cm) working single crochet, using a US size 7 (4.5mm) crochet hook and Cascade Yarns Spuntaneous Worsted.

### Abbreviations
See page 94.

### Special abbreviation
**MB (make bobble):** using yarn that is laid along top of row, [yarn over hook, insert hook in stitch, yarn round hook, pull yarn through work, yarn over hook, pull yarn through first 2 loops on hook] 6 times all in same stitch, using main color yarn over hook, pull through all loops on hook

## Pillow cover
Using US size 7 (4.5mm) hook and A, ch72.
**Row 1 (RS):** 1sc in second ch from hook, 1sc in each ch to end, turn. *(71 sts)*
**Rows 2–12:** Ch1 (does not count as st throughout), 1sc in each st to end, turn.
**Row 13 (bobble row 1):** Ch1, lay B along top of row as you work, using A, 1sc in each of next 5 sts, [using B, MB, using A, 1sc in each of next 11 sts] 5 times, using B, MB, using A, 1sc in each of next 5 sts.
**Rows 14–22:** Ch1, 1sc in each st to end.
**Row 23 (bobble row 2):** Ch1, lay B along top of row as you work, using A, 1sc in each of next 11 sts, [using B, MB, using A, 1sc in each of next 11 sts] 5 times.
**Rows 24–32:** As Rows 14–22.
Rep Rows 13–32 until work measures 25in (63cm), ending with a RS row.

## BORDER
**Round 1:** Work a second sc in last st of prev row (corner made), work 1sc in each row end down left-hand side, 2sc in corner st, work 1sc in each st along bottom edge, 2sc in corner st, work 1sc in each row end up right-hand side of pillow, 2sc in corner st, sl st in top of first st of last row of pillow to join.
Fasten off.

## Making up and finishing

Lay the pillow cover on a flat surface, RS down.
Place the pillow form in the middle, fold the bottom
of the cover up and the top of the cover down so that
the pillow form is enclosed, and the two edges overlap.
Pin across the join at the back of the pillow where
the opening will be. Pin the sides.

RUFFLE EDGE

**Row 1:** Using US size 7 (4.5mm) hook and A, work a sc
seam to join layers down one side, do not fasten off, turn.
**Row 2:** Ch1 (does not count as st throughout), 2sc in each
st to end, turn.
**Row 3:** Ch1, 2sc in each st to end.
Fasten off.
Rep on other side of pillow.

Sew in any ends (see page 87).
Stitch the three snap fasteners into place so that the
opening of the pillow is closed, and the fasteners are
hidden underneath the overlapping flap. Using a sewing
needle and thread, sew the three buttons onto the back
of the pillow, directly above where the fasteners are.

# Bobbly couch blanket

When the evenings get chilly, or you just fancy an afternoon curled up on the couch, this blanket is all you need to get cozy. Made in bulky yarn, it is beautifully warm and the pompoms add a contemporary twist to a simple blanket.

**SKILL LEVEL** ●●

### Yarn and materials
Paintbox Yarns Wool Mix Chunky (50% wool, 50% acrylic, 109yd/100m per 3½oz/100g ball) bulky (chunky) weight yarn:
    23 balls of Pistachio Green shade 1024 (A)

Paintbox Yarns Wool Mix Aran (50% wool, 50% acrylic, 197yd/180m per 3½oz/ 100g ball) worsted (aran) weight yarn:
    2 balls of Paper White shade 800 (B)

### Hook and equipment
US size J/10 (6mm) crochet hook

Yarn needle

1¾in (45mm) pompom maker

### Finished measurements
Width 44in (112cm), length 56in (142cm)

### Gauge (tension)
15 sts x 15 rows = 4¾ x 3½in (12 x 9cm) working single crochet, using a US size J/10 (6mm) crochet hook and Paintbox Yarns Wool Mix Chunky.

### Abbreviations
See page 94.

### Special abbreviation
**MB (make bobble):** using B, [yarn over hook, insert hook in stitch, yarn over hook, pull yarn through work, yarn over hook, pull yarn through first 2 loops on hook] 5 times all in same stitch, yarn over hook in A and pull through all loops on hook

## Blanket

Using A, ch144.

**Row 1:** 1sc in second ch from hook, 1sc in each ch to end, turn. *(143 sts)*

**Rows 2–6:** Ch1 (does not count as st throughout), 1sc in each of next 143 sts, turn.

***Row 7 (bobble row 1):** Ch1, lay B along top of row as you work, using A, 1sc in each of next 7 sts (working over B), using B, MB in next st, [using A, 1sc in each of next 15 sts, using B, MB in the next st] 8 times, using A, 1sc in each of last 7 sts.
Fasten off B at end of row.

**Rows 8–22:** Rep Row 2.

**Row 23 (bobble row 2):** Ch1, lay B along top of row as you work, [using A, 1sc in each of next 15 sts, using B, MB in next st] 8 times, using A, 1sc in each of last 15 sts.
Fasten off B at end of row.

**Rows 24–38:** Rep Row 2.**

Repeat from * to ** until you have worked a total of 14 bobble rows, ending with Bobble Row 2.
Work a further 6 rows of sc, ending on a RS row.
Do not fasten off, do not turn.

## BORDER

**Round 1:** Work a second sc in last st of row (corner made), work 1sc in each row end down left-hand side, 2sc in corner st, work 1sc in each st along bottom edge, 2sc in corner st, work 1sc in each row end up right-hand side of blanket, 2sc in corner st, sl st in top of first st of last row of blanket to join.

**Round 2:** Ch1, with RS still facing work crab st clockwise around edge of blanket as follows: [inserting hook from back to front, work 1sc in next st to the right] to end of round, sl st in ch-1 to join at end of round.
Fasten off.

## Making up and finishing

Sew in all ends (see page 87).
Using B and a 1¾in (45mm) pompom maker, make 18 pompoms, leaving a long tail on the central tie of each pompom. Attach 9 pompoms evenly along the top and bottom edge of the blanket.

~~~~~~~~~~~~~~~~~~~~~~~~~

**TIP** It will be easier to weave in the ends after attaching the pompoms if you use yarn A for the central tie, as then the ends will blend in with the main color of the blanket better.

# CHAPTER 3
# Wreaths & Garlands

# Daisy chain garland

If you have always wanted to make a crochet garland but have been a little overwhelmed at the prospect, this daisy chain garland couldn't be easier for your first attempt. The daisy petals are simple chains, attached to a circle in the center, and the leaves are created by working progressively longer stitches to create the shape. Each element has the exact same pattern, but by working them in different colorways you will create a detailed garland that looks more complicated than it actually is.

## SKILL LEVEL ●

### Yarn and materials
Cascade Yarns Ultra Pima (100% cotton, 220yd/200m per 3½oz/100g ball), light worsted (DK) weight yarn:
   1 ball in each of:
   Coral shade 3752 (A)
   Paprika shade 3771 (B)
   Zen Green shade 3757 (C)

### Hook and equipment
US size C/2-D/3 (3mm) crochet hook

Yarn needle

Hot glue gun or sewing needle and thread

### Finished measurements
Flowers: 1½in (4cm)

Leaves: 1⅜in (3.5cm)

Finished rope length: 43¼in (110cm)

### Gauge (tension)
Exact gauge is not important on this project.

### Abbreviations
See page 94.

## Daisies
(make 8 with B center and A petals, 15 with B center and C petals)

### CENTER
Using B, make a magic ring.
**Round 1:** 6sc into ring. *(6 sts)*
**Round 2:** [1sc in next st, 2sc in next st] 3 times, sl st in first st to join. *(9 sts)*
Fasten off.

### PETALS
**Round 3:** Join in either A or C to center with a sl st, ch10, sl st back in same st on center, *sl st in next st on center, ch10, sl st back in same st on center; rep from * 7 more times around center (9 petals), sl st in first st to join. Fasten off and sew in ends (see page 87).

## Leaves
(make 6 in C, 12 in B)
Using either B or C, ch9.
**Round 1:** Sl st in second ch from hook, 1sc in next ch, 1dc in each of next 4 ch, 1sc in next ch, 2sl st in next ch, cont working down opposite side of ch, 1sc in next ch, 1dc in each of next 4 ch, 1 sc in next ch, sl st in last ch, sl st in first st to join.
Fasten off and sew in ends.

## Hanging rope
Using 1 strand of A and 1 strand of B held tog, ch250.
Sl st in second ch from hook and in each ch to end.
Fasten off and sew in ends.

## Making up and finishing
Lay the rope on a flat surface so that it is taut and straight. If you are using a hot glue gun to attach your flowers and leaves you may wish to place some old card stock under the rope before you start the next step.
Now place the flowers and leaves in the position that you want them to be and, once you are happy with the arrangement, start sticking each piece to the rope with the hot glue gun. If you prefer you could stitch the flowers and leaves in place with a sewing needle and thread.

# Easter egg wreath

**For a change from chocolate eggs at Easter, try some pretty spotted crocheted ones instead! The two sizes of egg in bright spring colors and the large and small ivy leaves in green will welcome in those warmer days.**

## SKILL LEVEL ● ● ●

### Yarn and materials

Rowan Summerlite 4-ply (100% cotton, 191yd/175m per 1¾oz/50g ball) fingering (4-ply) weight yarn:
   1 ball in each of:
   Sandstone shade 435 (A)
   Ecru shade 436 (B)
   Pinched Pink shade 426 (C)

Rowan Cotton Glacé (100% cotton, 125yd/115m per 1¾oz/50g ball) light worsted (DK) weight yarn
   1 ball of Shoot shade 814 (D)

1½in (40mm) polystyrene eggs (optional)

1¼in (30mm) polystyrene eggs (optional)

Polyester toy fiberfill (if not using polystyrene eggs)

10in (25cm) diameter pale wicker wreath

Ribbon

### Hook and equipment

US size B/1–C/2 (2.5mm) crochet hook

Yarn needle

Stitch marker

Pins

Hot glue gun

### Finished measurements

Wreath: 10in (25cm) diameter

### Gauge (tension)

15 sts x 15 rows = 2¼in (6cm) square working single crochet, using a US size B/1–C/2 (2.5mm) crochet hook.

### Abbreviations

See page 94.

## Wreath

### LARGE IVY LEAF (MAKE 5 IN D)

**Round 1:** Using D, make a magic ring, 5sc into the ring.
Work in a continuous spiral. PM in last st and move up as each round is finished.
**Round 2:** 2sc in each st to end. *(10 sc)*
**Round 3:** *1sc, 2sc in next st; rep from * to end, sl st in first st to join. *(15 sc)*
**Point 1:** Ch4, sl st in second ch from hook, 1sc, 1hdc, miss next st of center, sl st in next st.
**Point 2:** Ch5, sl st in second ch from hook, 1sc, 1hdc, 1dc, miss next st of center, sl st in next st.
**Point 3:** Ch7, sl st in second ch from hook, 1sc, 1hdc, 1dc, 1tr, 1dtr, miss 2 sts of center, sl st in next st of center.
**Point 4:** Rep point 2.
**Point 5:** Rep point 1.
**Stem:** Sl st in next st, ch5, sl st in second ch from hook, sl st in each of next 3 ch, sl st in base of 5-ch.
Fasten off.

### SMALL IVY LEAF (MAKE 8 IN D)

**Round 1:** Using D, make a magic ring, 4sc into the ring.
Work in a continuous spiral. PM in last st and move up as each round is finished.
**Round 2:** 2sc in each st to end. *(8 sc)*
**Round 3:** *1sc, 2sc in next st; rep from * to end, sl st in first st to join. *(12 sc)*
**Point 1:** Ch3, sl st in second ch from hook, 1sc, sl st in next st.
**Point 2:** Ch4, sl st in second ch from hook, 1sc, 1hdc, miss next st of center, sl st in next st.
**Point 3:** Ch6, sl st in second ch from hook, 1sc, 1hdc, 1dc, 1tr, miss 2 sts of center, sl st in next st.
**Point 4:** Rep point 2.
**Point 5:** Rep point 1.
**Stem:** Sl st in next st, ch5, sl st in second ch from hook, sl st in each of next 3 ch, sl st in base of 5-ch.
Fasten off.

~~~~~~~~~~~~~

**Tip** The eggs on the wreath can be made in two different ways—either by adding a polystyrene egg halfway through or by stuffing the egg with toy fiberfill. Both ways work equally well.

## SMALL EGG (MAKE 1 IN B, 2 IN C)

**Round 1:** Using B or C, make a magic ring, 4sc into the ring. Work in a continuous spiral. PM in last st and move up as each round is finished.

**Round 2:** 2sc in each st to end. *(8 sts)*

**Round 3:** *1sc, 2sc in next st; rep from * to end. *(12 sts)*

**Round 4:** *1sc in each of next 2 sts, 2sc in next st; rep from * to end. *(16 sts)*

**Rounds 5 and 6:** 1sc in each st to end.

**Round 7:** *1sc in each of next 3 sts, 2sc in next st; rep from * to end. *(20 sts)*

**Round 8:** *1sc in each of next 4 sts, 2sc in next st; rep from * to end. *(24 sts)*

**Rounds 9 and 10:** 1sc in each st. *(24 sts)*

Insert polystyrene egg (optional).

**Round 11:** *1sc in each of next 4 sts, sc2tog; rep from * to end. *(20 sts)*

**Round 12:** *1sc in each of next 3 sts, sc2tog; rep from * to end. *(16 sts)*

**Round 13:** *1sc in each of next 2 sts, sc2tog; rep from * to end. *(12 sts)*

If not using polystyrene egg, insert fiberfill.

**Round 14:** *1sc, sc2tog; rep from * to end. *(8 sts)*

**Round 15:** [Sc2tog] to end.

Fasten off.

## Making up and finishing

Block the ivy leaves.

To finish the eggs, work some French knots (see page 90) all over each egg in contrasting colors.

Lay the wreath on a flat surface and use blocking pins to position and pin the blocked ivy leaves and eggs where you want them to be. Glue firmly in place with a hot glue gun.

To finish off the wreath, stitch or glue a coordinating ribbon and hanging loop at the top.

## LARGE EGG (MAKE 3 IN A, 1 IN B, 1 IN C)

**Round 1:** Using A, B or C, make a magic ring, 4sc into the ring.

Work in a continuous spiral. PM in last st and move up as each round is finished.

**Round 2:** 2sc in each st to end. *(8 sts)*

**Round 3:** *1sc, 2sc in next st; rep from * to end. *(12 sts)*

**Round 4:** *1sc in each of next 2 sts, 2sc in next st; rep from * to end. *(16 sts)*

**Round 5:** *1sc in each of next 3 sts, 2sc in next st; rep from * to end. *(20 sts)*

**Rounds 6 and 7:** 1sc in each st to end. *(20 sts)*

**Round 8:** *1sc in each of next 4 sts, 2sc in next st; rep from * to end. *(24 sts)*

**Rounds 9 to 12:** 1sc in each st to end.

Insert polystyrene egg (optional).

**Round 13:** *1sc in each of next 4 sts, sc2tog; rep from * to end. *(20 sts)*

**Round 14:** *1sc in each of next 3 sts, sc2tog; rep from * to end. *(16 sts)*

**Round 15:** *1sc in each of next 2 sts, sc2tog; rep from * to end. *(12 sts)*

If not using polystyrene egg, insert fiberfill.

**Round 16:** *1sc, sc2tog; rep from * to end. *(8 sts)*

**Round 17:** [Sc2tog] to end.

Fasten off.

# Heart garland

This little heart garland looks perfect strung above a mirror or a chest of drawers, and can be made in any color combination to match your décor. As a finishing touch, small brass jingle bells add a beautiful musical note when caught by the breeze.

**SKILL LEVEL** ●●

### Yarn and materials

Rowan Cotton Glacé (100% cotton, 125yd/115m per 1¾oz/50g ball) DK (light worsted) weight yarn:

    1 ball in each of:
    Oyster shade 730 (A)
    Ecru shade 725 (B)
    Dawn Gray shade 831 (C)

Polyester toy fiberfill

64in (160cm) of narrow cord/ribbon

Short lengths of ribbon for heart hanging loops

10 jingle bells, ½in (10mm) size

Short lengths of ribbon for attaching the bells

### Hook and equipment

US size C/2-D/3 (3mm) crochet hook

Stitch marker

### Finished measurements

Each heart: approx. 2¾ x 2¾in (7 x 7cm) at widest point

Garland: approx. 45in (114cm) long

### Gauge (tension)

15 sts x 15 rows = 2¾ x 2½in (7 x 6.5cm) working single crochet, using a US size C/2-D/3 (3mm) crochet hook.

### Abbreviations

See page 94.

## Garland

### HEART (MAKE 2 IN A, 2 IN B, 3 IN C)

Heart lobes (make 2 for each heart)

**Round 1:** Using A, B or C, make a magic ring, 5sc into the ring.

Work in a continuous spiral. PM in last st and move up as each round is finished.

**Round 2:** 2sc in each st to end. *(10 sts)*

**Round 3:** *1sc, 2sc in next st; rep from * to end. *(15 sts)*

**Round 4:** *1sc in each of first 2 sts, 2sc in next st; rep from * to end. *(20 sts)*

**Rounds 5–8:** 1sc in each st to end.

On first lobe, join with a sl st at end of Round 8 and fasten off.

On second lobe, do not join with sl st or fasten off.

**Joining the lobes:**

Holding second lobe, place first lobe next to it so first side is nearest to you. Flatten both lobes so four edges are together. Join two inner edges only with a sc seam, working 6sc so seam is on inside of completed heart. PM in last st of seam. This will mark the beg/end of round. Move it up as indicated on each round as you work in a continuous spiral.

**Round 9:** Beg from marked st, work 1sc in each st around two sides of heart (approx. 35 sts, alter st count in next round if needed).

**Round 10:** 1sc in each st, inc or dec as necessary to 34 sts, PM in last st.

**Round 11:** 1sc in each of next 6 sts, sc2tog, 1sc in each of next 16 sts, sc2tog, 1sc in each of next 8 sts. PM in last st. *(32 sts)*

**Round 12:** 1sc in each of next 6 sts, sc2tog, 1sc in each of next 7 sts, sc2tog, 1sc in each of next 6 sts, sc2tog, 1sc in each of next 7 sts, PM in last st. *(29 sts)*

**Round 13:** 1sc in each of next 6 sts, sc2tog, 1sc in each of next 6 sts, sc2tog, 1sc in each of next 5 sts, sc2tog, 1sc in each of next 5 sts (1 st before marker), sc2tog, PM in last st. *(25 sts)*

**Round 14:** 1sc in each of next 5 sts, sc2tog, 1sc in each of next 5 sts, sc2tog, 1sc in each of next 4 sts, sc2tog, 1sc in each of next 4 sts, (1 st before marker), sc2tog, PM in last st. *(21 sts)*

**Round 15:** 1sc in each of next 10 sts, sc2tog, 1sc in each of next 8 sts (1 st before marker), sc2tog. *(19 sts)*

You may find it easier to work without the marker from this point onward.

Stuff heart lobes.

**Round 16:** 1sc in each of next 9 sts, sc2tog, 1sc in each of next 7 sts, sc2tog. *(17 sts)*

**Round 17:** 1sc in each of next 3 sts, sc2tog, 1sc in each of next 3 sts, sc2tog, 1sc in each of next 2 sts, sc2tog, 1sc in each of last 2 sts. *(14 sts)*

**Round 18:** Sc2tog, 1sc in each of next 2 sts, sc2tog, 1sc in each of next 2 sts, sc2tog, 1sc, sc2tog, 1sc, sc2tog. *(9 sts)*

Finish stuffing heart.

**Round 19:** 1sc, sc2tog, 1sc, sc2tog, 1sc, sc2tog, 1sc, sc2tog. Close rem hole with sl st, fasten off.

## Making up and finishing

Sew in all ends (see page 87).

Using a needle and matching thread, sew a ribbon hanging loop to the top of each heart, between the two heart tips. Thread the hearts onto the garland ribbon/cord and stitch in place with a needle and thread to stop them slipping along the cord.

Add a small ribbon loop to each bell and sew one between each heart as a finishing touch.

**TIP** The hearts are worked from the top downward. You'll make the curved lobes at the top in two separate domes, and then join them in the center and work down to the point in rounds.

# Wish upon a star wreath

Whether for a child's bedroom or as an addition to your holiday decorations, this wreath is designed with simplicity and understatement in mind. The three different-sized stars have been added to a dark twig wreath to make them stand out for full effect. To give each star extra twinkle a strand of metallic thread has been worked in with the yarn.

**SKILL LEVEL** ●

## Yarn and materials
James C. Brett Twinkle DK
(3% polyester, 97% acrylic, 328yd/
300m per 3½oz/100g ball) light worsted
(DK) weight yarn:
  1 ball in each of:
  Silver shade TK8 (A)
  White shade TK2 (B)

Drops Glitter Thread (765yd/
700m per ½oz/10g spool) yarn
  1 spool of Silver shade 02 (C)

12in (30cm) diameter twig wreath

Coordinating ribbon

## Hook and equipment
US size B/1 (2mm) crochet hook

Stitch marker

Pins

Hot glue gun

## Finished measurements
Each large star: approx. 2¼in (5.5cm) wide

Wreath: 12in (30cm) diameter

## Gauge (tension)
15 sts x 15 rows = 2¼in (6cm) square
working single crochet, using a
US size B/1 (2mm) crochet hook.

## Abbreviations
See page 94.

## Wreath

### LARGE STAR (MAKE 2 IN A, 1 IN B)
**Round 1:** Using A or B held tog with C, make a magic ring, 5sc into the ring.
Work in a continuous spiral. PM in last st and move up as each round is finished.
**Round 2:** 2sc in each st to end. *(10 sts)*
**Round 3:** *1sc, 2sc in next st; rep from * 4 more times, sl st in first st to join. *(15 sts)*
**Round 4:** *Ch7, sl st in second ch from hook, 1sc, 1hdc, 2dc in next ch, miss last 2 ch and next 2 sts of center, sl st in next st; rep from * 4 more times around (5 points), ending last point with sl st in base of first point.
Fasten off.

### MEDIUM STAR (MAKE 4 IN A, 4 IN B)
**Round 1:** Using A or B held tog with C, make a magic ring, 5sc into the ring.
Work in a continuous spiral, do not join.
**Round 2:** 2sc in each st to end, sl st in first st to join. *(10 sts)*
**Round 3:** *Ch5, sl st in second ch from hook, 1sc, 1hdc, miss last ch and next st of center, sl st in next st; rep from * 4 more times around (5 points), ending last point with sl st in base of first point.
Fasten off.

### SMALL STAR (MAKE 3 IN A, 2 IN B)
**Round 1:** Using A or B held tog with C, make a magic ring, 5sc into the ring, sl st in first st to join.
**Round 2:** *Ch4, sl st in second ch from hook, 1sc, miss last ch, sl st in next st of center; rep from * 4 more times around (5 points), ending last point with sl st in base of first point.
Fasten off.

## Making up and finishing
Block the stars.
Lay the wreath on a flat surface. Use blocking pins to position the blocked stars where you want them to be. Glue firmly in place with a hot glue gun.
To finish off the wreath, add a bow in a coordinating color by attaching it with a glue gun.

**TIP** To give your wreath a more festive feel, use a red glitter yarn such as James C. Brett Twinkle DK in Red shade TK20, to make the stars.

# Bobbly heart wreath

This bobbly heart wreath could not be simpler to make. It adds a beautiful touch to any room in the house, with the bobble color being easy to change to coordinate with any décor. The bobbles are threaded onto a length of elastic thread, making it easier to attach them to the wreath base.

## SKILL LEVEL ●

### Yarn and materials
Sirdar Cashmere Merino Silk DK (75% merino wool, 20% silk, 5% cashmere, 127yd/116m per 1¾oz/ 50g ball) light worsted (DK) weight yarn:
  1 ball in each of:
  Waterlily shade 401 (A)
  Silver Gray shade 405 (B)
  Mother of Pearl shade 408 (C)
  Regency Blue shade 400 (D)

Polyester toy fiberfill

Elastic thread

10½ x 10in (26 x 25cm) wicker heart

Ribbon for hanging loop

### Hook and equipment
US size C/2-D/3 (3mm) crochet hook

Stitch marker

Yarn needle

Pins

Hot glue gun

### Finished measurements
Each bobble: approx. 1in (2.5cm) diameter

Wreath: 10½ x 10in (26 x 25cm)

### Gauge (tension)
15 sts x 15 rows = 2½ x 2¼in (6.5 x 6cm) working single crochet, using a US size C/2-D/3 (3mm) crochet hook.

### Abbreviations
See page 94.

## Wreath

### BOBBLE (MAKE 9 IN A, C AND D, 10 IN B)
**Round 1:** Using A, B, C or D, make a magic ring, 4sc into the ring.
Work in a continuous spiral. PM in last st and move up as each round is finished.
**Round 2:** 2sc in each st to end. *(8 sts)*
**Round 3:** *1sc, 2sc in next st; rep from * to end. *(12 sts)*
**Round 4:** *1sc in each of next 2 sts, 2sc in next st; rep from * to end. *(16 sts)*
**Round 5:** 1sc in each st to end.
**Round 6:** *1sc in each of next 2 sts, sc2tog; rep from * to end. *(12 sts)*
**Round 7:** *1sc in next st, sc2tog; rep from * to end. *(8 sts)*
Stuff the bobble.
**Round 8:** [Sc2tog] to end. *(4 sts)*
Fasten off, using long end to gather and close hole.

## Making up and finishing
Keeping the color sequence correct, thread each bobble onto the elastic thread. Once all the bobbles are joined together, position them on the wreath base, holding with blocking pins. Stick the string of bobbles to the wreath with a hot glue gun.
Attach a hanging loop made with coordinating ribbon.

# Simple Easter garland

This alternative Easter garland is made up of chicken's eggs and fresh spring carrots! Each item is tied onto a rustic piece of rope for a simple, fresh look—perfect for hanging in your kitchen.

## SKILL LEVEL ●

### Yarn and materials

Rowan Summerlite DK (100% cotton, 142yd/130m per 1¾oz/50g ball) light worsted (DK) weight yarn:
  1 ball in each of:
  Linen shade 460 (A)
  Pear shade 463 (B)
  Cantaloupe shade 456 (C)

Polyester toy fiberfill

11 short lengths of thin string

60in (1.5m) of cord or thin rope

6 short lengths of green ribbon

### Hook and equipment

US size B/1–C/2 (2.5mm) crochet hook

Stitch marker

Yarn needle

### Finished measurements

Carrot: approx. 4in (10cm) long

Egg: approx. 2in (5cm) long

Garland: approx. 52in (130cm) long

### Gauge (tension)

15 sts x 15 rows = 2¼in (6cm) square working single crochet, using a US size B/1–C/2 (2.5mm) crochet hook.

### Abbreviations

See page 94.

## Garland

### EGG (MAKE 7)

**Round 1:** Using A, make a magic ring, 4sc into the ring.
Work in a continuous spiral. PM in last st and move up as each round is finished.
**Round 2:** 2sc in each st to end. *(8 sts)*
**Round 3:** *1sc, 2sc in next st; rep from * to end. *(12 sts)*
**Round 4:** *1sc in each of next 2 sts, 2sc in next st; rep from * to end. *(16 sts)*
**Rounds 5 and 6:** 1sc in each st to end.
**Round 7:** *1sc in each of next 3 sts, 2sc in next st; rep from * to end. *(20 sts)*
**Round 8:** *1sc in each of next 4 sts, 2sc in next st; rep from * to end. *(24 sts)*
**Rounds 9 and 10:** 1sc in each st to end.
Stuff top of egg.
**Round 11:** *1sc in each of next 4 sts, sc2tog; rep from * to end. *(20 sts)*
**Round 12:** *1sc in each of next 3 sts, sc2tog; rep from * to end. *(16 sts)*
**Round 13:** *1sc in each of next 2 sts, sc2tog; rep from * to end. *(12 sts)*
**Round 14:** *1sc, sc2tog; rep from * to end. *(8 sts)*
Finish stuffing egg.
**Round 15:** [Sc2tog] to end.
Fasten off.

### CARROT (MAKE 5)

**Round 1:** Using C, make a magic ring, 4sc into the ring.
Work in a continuous spiral. PM in last st and move up as each round is finished.
**Round 2:** *1sc, 2sc in next st; rep from * to end. *(6 sts)*

**Round 3:** 1sc in each st to end.
**Round 4:** *1sc, 2sc in next st; rep from * to end. *(9 sts)*
**Round 5:** 1sc in each st to end.
**Round 6:** *1sc, 2sc in next st; rep from * 3 more times, 1sc. *(13 sts)*
**Round 7:** 1sc in each st to end.
**Round 8:** *1sc in each of next 2 sts, 2sc in next st; rep from * 3 more times, 2sc in next st. *(18 sts)*
**Round 9:** 1sc in each st to end.
**Round 10:** *1sc in each of next 3 sts, 2sc in next st; rep from * 3 more times, 1sc in each of next 2 sts. *(22 sts)*
**Rounds 11 to 18:** 1sc in each st to end.
**Round 19:** *2sc, sc2tog; rep from * 4 more times, 2sc. *(17 sts)*
**Round 20:** *1sc, sc2tog; rep from * 4 more times, 2sc. *(12 sts)*
Stuff carrot.
**Round 21:** [Sc2tog] to end. *(6 sts)*
Gather up rem hole to close, then fasten off.
To finish the carrot, join B to center top of carrot with a sl st, *ch11, sl st in each of next 11 ch, join with a sl st in center top of carrot; rep from * 4 more times. Fasten off.

## Making up and finishing

Thread a length of thin string into the top of each carrot and egg and hang each item onto the length of rope to form your garland. Tie a small bow in green ribbon above each egg.

# Mistletoe wreath

**This stylish and simple wreath will add a festive feel to any room over the holiday season—and with the leaves being quick and simple to make you'll find yourself making them for friends and loved ones, too!**

## SKILL LEVEL ●

### Yarn and materials
James C Brett Twinkle DK
(3% polyester, 97% acrylic, 328yd/
300m per 3½oz/100g ball) light
worsted (DK) weight yarn:
   1 ball in each of:
   Green shade TK37 (A)
   White shade TK2 (B)

10in (25cm) diameter wicker wreath,
sprayed with artificial snow

Ribbon for a hanging loop

### Hook and equipment
US size C/2–D/3 (3mm) crochet hook

Yarn needle

Hot glue gun

### Finished measurements
Wreath: 10in (25cm) diameter

Each mistletoe (beg of stem
to tip of leaf): 2¾in (7cm)

### Gauge (tension)
15 sts x 15 rows = 2¾ x 2½in
(7 x 6.5cm) working single
crochet, using a US size C/2–D/3
(3mm) crochet hook.

### Abbreviations
See page 94.

## Wreath

MISTLETOE (MAKE 10)
Using A, ch11.
**Leaf 1:** Sl st in second ch from hook,
sl st in each of next 3 ch, 1sc in each
of next 4 ch, 1hdc, 2hdc in the last ch,
do not turn, working back down other
side of ch, 1hdc in each of first 4 ch,
1sc in each of next 3 ch, sl st in each
of last 3 ch.
**Stalk:** Ch12, sl st in second ch from
hook, sl st in each of next 10 ch, ending
at base of leaf 1.
**Leaf 2:** Ch11, 1hdc in second ch from
hook, 1hdc in each of next 4 ch, 1sc
in each of next 3 ch, sl st in each of last
2 ch, do not turn, ch1, working back
down other side of ch, miss first ch,
sl st in each of next 2 ch, 1sc in each
of next 4 ch, 1hdc in each of last 3 ch,
sl st in first st to join.
Fasten off.

## Making up and finishing
To complete each mistletoe sprig,
embroider 2 to 3 French knots (see
page 90) in B where the two leaves
meet at the bottom. The knots will
also serve to hold the leaves together.
Use a hot glue gun to stick the leaves
into position. Finish the wreath
by adding a hanging loop in
coordinating ribbon.

# Techniques

In this section, we explain how to master the simple crochet and finishing techniques that you need to make the projects in this book.

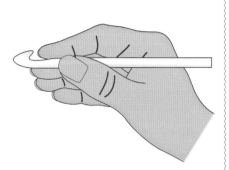

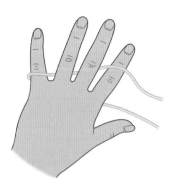

## Holding the hook

Pick up your hook as though you are picking up a pen or pencil. Keeping the hook held loosely between your fingers and thumb, turn your hand so that the palm is facing up and the hook is balanced in your hand and resting in the space between your index finger and your thumb.

You can also hold the hook like a knife—this may be easier if you are working with a large hook or with bulky yarn. Choose the method that you find most comfortable.

## Holding the yarn

**1** Pick up the yarn with your little finger in the opposite hand to your hook, with your palm facing upward and with the short end in front. Turn your hand to face downward, with the yarn on top of your index finger and under the other two fingers and wrapped right around the little finger, as shown above.

**2** Turn your hand to face you, ready to hold the work in your middle finger and thumb. Keeping your index finger only at a slight curve, hold the work or the slip knot using the same hand, between your middle finger and your thumb and just below the crochet hook and loop/s on the hook.

## Holding the hook and yarn while crocheting

Keep your index finger, with the yarn draped over it, at a slight curve, and hold your work (or the slip knot) using the same hand, between your middle finger and your thumb and just below the crochet hook and loop/s on the hook.

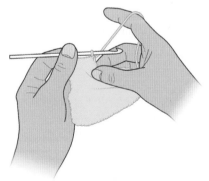

As you draw the loop through the hook release the yarn on the index finger to allow the loop to stay loose on the hook. If you tense your index finger, the yarn will become too tight and pull the loop on the hook too tight for you to draw the yarn through.

## Holding the hook and yarn for left-handers

Some left-handers learn to crochet like right-handers, but others learn with everything reversed—with the hook in the left hand and the yarn in the right.

## Making a slip knot

The simplest way is to make a circle with the yarn, so that the loop is facing downward.

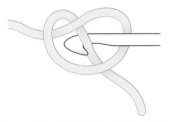

**1** In one hand hold the circle at the top where the yarn crosses, and let the tail drop down at the back so that it falls across the center of the loop. With your free hand or the tip of a crochet hook, pull a loop through the circle.

**2** Put the hook into the loop and pull gently so that it forms a loose loop on the hook.

## Yarn over hook (yoh)

To create a stitch, catch the yarn from behind with the hook pointing upward. As you gently pull the yarn through the loop on the hook, turn the hook so it faces downward and slide the yarn through the loop. The loop on the hook should be kept loose enough for the hook to slide through easily.

## Magic ring

This is a useful starting technique if you do not want a visible hole in the center of your round. Loop the yarn around your finger, insert the hook through the ring, yarn over hook, pull through the ring to make the first chain. Work the number of stitches required into the ring and then pull the end to tighten the center ring and close the hole.

## Chain (ch)

**1** Using the hook, wrap the yarn over the hook ready to pull it through the loop on the hook.

**2** Pull through, creating a new loop on the hook. Continue in this way to create a chain of the required length.

## Chain ring

If you are crocheting a round shape, one way of starting off is by crocheting a number of chains following the instructions in your pattern, and then joining them into a circle.

**1** To join the chain into a circle, insert the crochet hook into the first chain that you made (not into the slip knot), yarn over hook.

**2** Pull the yarn through the chain and through the loop on your hook at the same time, thereby creating a slip stitch and forming a circle. You now have a chain ring ready to work stitches into as instructed in the pattern.

## Chain space (ch sp)

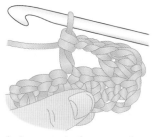

**1** A chain space is the space that has been made under a chain in the previous round or row, and falls in between other stitches.

**2** Stitches into a chain space are made directly into the hole created under the chain and not into the chain stitches themselves.

## Slip stitch (sl st)

A slip stitch doesn't create any height and is often used as the last stitch to create a smooth and even round or row.

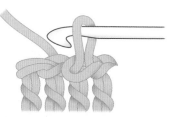

**1** To make a slip stitch: first put the hook through the work, yarn round hook.

**2** Pull the yarn through both the work and through the loop on the hook at the same time, so you will have 1 loop on the hook.

## Making rounds

When working in rounds the work is not turned, so you are always working from one side. Depending on the pattern you are working, a "round" can be square.

Start each round by making one or more chains to create the height you need for the stitch you are working:

Single crochet = 1 chain
Half double crochet = 2 chains
Double crochet = 3 chains
Treble crochet = 4 chains
Double treble crochet = 5 chains

Work the required stitches to complete the round. At the end of the round, slip stitch into the top of the chain to close the round.

## Continuous spiral

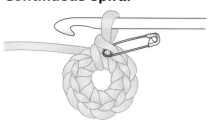

If you work in a spiral you do not need a turning chain. After completing the base ring, place a stitch marker in the first stitch and then continue to crochet around. When you have made a round and reached the point where the stitch marker is, work this stitch, take out the stitch marker from the previous round and put it back into the first stitch of the new round. A safety pin or piece of yarn in a contrasting color makes a good stitch marker.

## Making rows

When making straight rows you turn the work at the end of each row and make a turning chain to create the height you need for the stitch you are working with, as for making rounds.

Single crochet = 1 chain
Half double crochet = 2 chains
Double crochet = 3 chains
Treble crochet = 4 chains
Double treble crochet = 5 chains

## Working into top of stitch

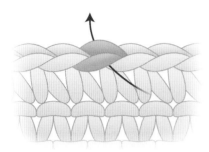

Unless otherwise directed, always insert the hook under both of the two loops on top of the stitch—this is the standard technique.

To work into the front loop of a stitch, pick up the front loop from underneath at the front of the work.

## Working into front loop of stitch (FLO)

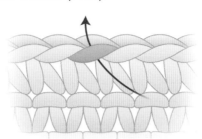

To work into the front loop of a stitch, pick up the front loop from underneath at the front of the work.

## Working into back loop of stitch (BLO)

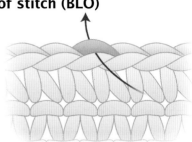

To work into the back loop of the stitch, insert the hook between the front and the back loop, picking up the back loop from the front of the work.

## How to measure a gauge (tension) square

Using the hook and the yarn recommended in the pattern, make a number of chains to measure approximately 6in (15cm). Working in the stitch pattern given for the gauge measurements, work enough rows to form a square. Fasten off.

Take a ruler, place it horizontally across the square and, using pins, mark a 4in (10cm) area. Repeat vertically to form a 4in (10cm) square on the fabric. Count the number of stitches across, and the number of rows within the square, and compare against the gauge given in the pattern.

If your numbers match the pattern then use this size hook and yarn for your project. If you have more stitches, then your gauge is tighter than recommended and you need to use a larger hook. If you have fewer stitches, then your gauge is looser and you will need a smaller hook.

Make gauge squares using different size hooks until you have matched the gauge in the pattern, and use this hook to make the project.

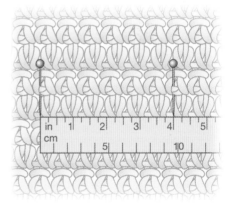

## Single crochet (sc)

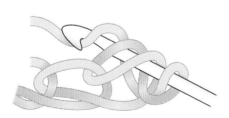

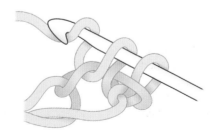

**1** Insert the hook into your work, yarn over hook and pull the yarn through the work only. You will then have 2 loops on the hook.

**2** Yarn over hook again and pull through the two loops on the hook. You will then have 1 loop on the hook.

## Half double crochet (hdc)

  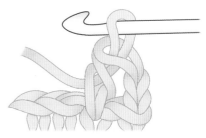

**1** Before inserting the hook into the work, wrap the yarn over the hook, and put the hook through the work with the yarn wrapped around.

**2** Yarn over hook again and pull through the first loop on the hook. You now have 3 loops on the hook.

**3** Yarn over hook and pull the yarn through all 3 loops. You will be left with 1 loop on the hook.

## Double crochet (dc)

  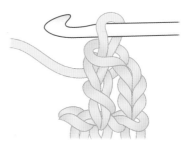

**1** Before inserting the hook into the work, wrap the yarn over the hook. Put the hook through the work with the yarn wrapped around, yarn over hook again, and pull through the first loop on the hook. You now have 3 loops on the hook.

**2** Yarn over hook again, pull the yarn through the first 2 loops on the hook. You now have 2 loops on the hook.

**3** Pull the yarn through 2 loops again. You will be left with 1 loop on the hook.

## Treble (tr)

Yarn over hook twice, insert the hook into the stitch, yarn over hook, pull a loop through (4 loops on hook), yarn over hook, pull the yarn through 2 stitches (3 loops on hook), yarn over hook, pull a loop through the next 2 stitches (2 loops on hook), yarn over hook, pull a loop through the last 2 stitches. You will be left with 1 loop on the hook.

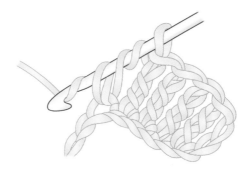

## Double treble (dtr)

Double trebles are "tall" stitches and are an extension on the basic double crochet stitch. They need a turning chain of 5 chains.

**1** Yarn over hook three times, insert the hook into the stitch or space. Yarn over hook, pull the yarn through the work (5 loops on hook).

**2** Yarn over hook, pull the yarn through the first 2 loops on the hook (4 loops on hook).

**3** Yarn over hook, pull the yarn through the first 2 loops on the hook (3 loops on hook).

**4** Yarn over hook, pull the yarn through the first 2 loops on the hook (2 loops on hook). Yarn over hook, pull the yarn through the 2 loops on the hook. You will be left with 1 loop on the hook.

---

## Front post double crochet (FPdc)

Raised stitches are created by making stitches around the "posts"—or "stems"—of the stitches in the previous row/round. Here the stitches are being worked around to the front.

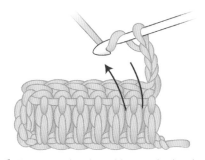 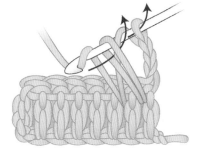 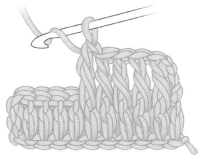

**1** Yarn over hook and insert the hook from the front and around the post (the stem) of the next double crochet from right to left.

**2** Yarn over hook and pull the yarn through the work, yarn over hook, and pull the yarn through the first 2 loops on the hook.

**3** Yarn over hook and pull the yarn through the 2 loops on the hook (1 loop on the hook).

## Bobble

Bobbles are created when working on wrong-side rows and the bobble is then pushed out toward the right-side row. This is a four-double crochet cluster bobble (4dcCL).

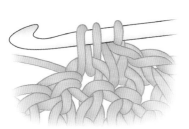

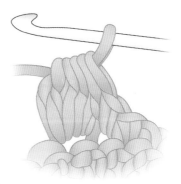

**1** Yarn over hook and then insert the hook in the stitch, yarn over hook, and pull the yarn through the work.

**2** Yarn over hook and pull the yarn through the first 2 loops on the hook (2 loops on hook).

**3** Repeat steps 1 and 2 three more times in the same stitch, yarn over hook, and pull through all 5 loops on the hook.

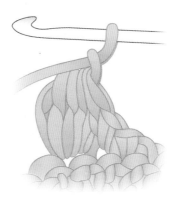

**4** You can also make 1 chain to complete the bobble.

## Picots

A picot is a little bobble texture that is often used to create decorative little points along the outer edge of an edging. This sample shows how to make a 3ch-picot, but follow the instructions in the pattern for the number of chains to make.

**1** Make 14ch.
**Row 1:** 1sc in second ch from hook, 1sc in each ch to end.
**Row 2:** 1ch, 1sc in each of next 2 sts, 3dc in next st, *1sc in each of the next 3 sts, 3dc in next st: rep from * twice more, 2sc in each of last 2 sts.
**Row 3 (picot row):** 1ch, 1sc in each of next 2 sc, 1sc in top of next dc, *3ch.

**2** Sl st in third ch from hook (one picot made), 1sc in top of next dc.

**3** Rep from * once more, 3ch, sl st in third ch from hook (picot made)**, 1sc in each of next 3 sc, 1sc in top of next dc; rep from * ending last rep at **, 1sc in each of last two sc.

## Increasing

Make two or three stitches into one stitch or space from the previous row. The illustration shows a double crochet increase being made.

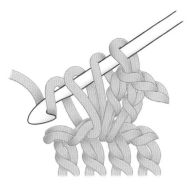

## Decreasing

You can decrease by either missing the next stitch and continuing to crochet, or by crocheting two or more stitches together. The basic technique for crocheting stitches together is the same, no matter which stitch you are using. The following example shows sc2tog.

## Single crochet two stitches together (sc2tog)

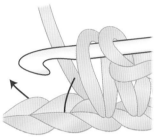 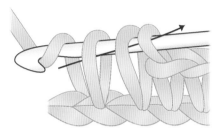

**1** Insert the hook into your work, yarn over hook, and pull the yarn through the work (2 loops on hook). Insert the hook in next stitch, yarn over hook, and pull the yarn through.

**2** Yarn over hook again and pull through all 3 loops on the hook. You will then have 1 loop on the hook.

## Joining yarn at the end of a row or round

You can use this technique when changing color, or when joining in a new ball of yarn as one runs out.

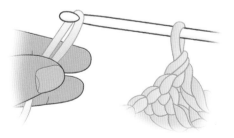 

**1** Keep the loop of the old yarn on the hook. Drop the tail and catch a loop of the strand of the new yarn with the crochet hook.

**2** Draw the new yarn through the loop on the hook, keeping the old loop drawn tight, and continue as instructed in the pattern.

## Joining in new yarn after fastening off

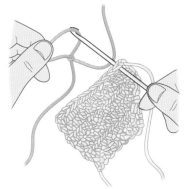

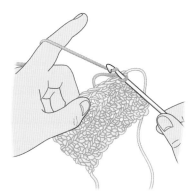

**1** Fasten off the old color (see page 87). Make a slip knot with the new color (see page 79). Insert the hook into the stitch at the beginning of the next row, then through the slip knot.

**2** Draw the loop of the slip knot through to the front of the work. Carry on working using the new color, following the instructions in the pattern.

## Joining yarn in the middle of a row or round

For a neat color join in the middle of a row or round, use these methods.

### Joining a new color into single crochet

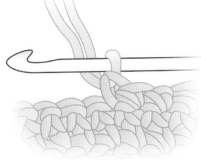

**1** Make a single crochet stitch (see page 81), but do not draw the final loop through, so there are 2 loops on the hook. Drop the old yarn, catch the new yarn with the hook, and draw it through both loops to complete the stitch and join in the new color at the same time.

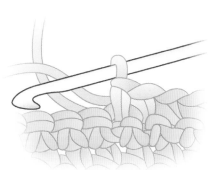

**2** Continue to crochet with the new yarn. Cut the old yarn leaving a 6in (15cm) tail and weave the tail in (see right) after working a row, or once the work is complete.

### Joining a new color into double crochet

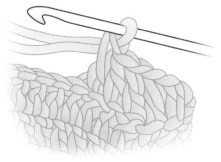

**1** Make a double crochet stitch (see page 82), but do not draw the final loop through, so there are 2 loops on the hook. Drop the old yarn, catch the new yarn with the hook, and draw it through both loops to complete the stitch and join in the new color at the same time.

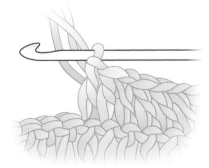

**2** Continue to crochet with the new yarn. Cut the old yarn leaving a 6in (15cm) tail and weave the tail in (see right) after working a row, or once the work is complete.

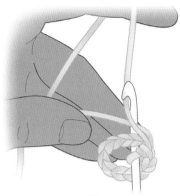

## Enclosing a yarn tail

You may find that the yarn tail gets in the way as you work; you can enclose this into the stitches as you go by placing the tail at the back as you wrap the yarn. This also saves having to sew this tail end in later.

## Fastening off

When you have finished crocheting, you need to fasten off the stitches to stop all your work unraveling.

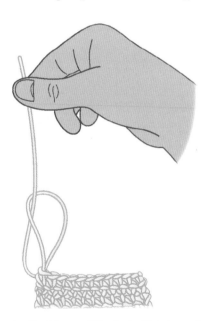

**1** Draw up the final loop of the last stitch to make it bigger. Cut the yarn, leaving a tail of approximately 4in (10cm)—unless a longer end is needed for sewing up. Pull the tail all the way through the loop and pull the loop up tightly.

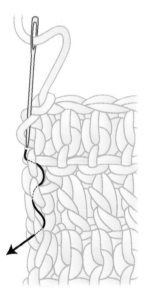

## Weaving in yarn ends

It is important to weave in the tail ends of the yarn so that they are secure and your crochet won't unravel. Thread a yarn needle with the tail end of yarn. On the wrong side, take the needle through the crochet one stitch down on the edge, then take it through the stitches, working in a gentle zig-zag. Work through four or five stitches then return in the opposite direction. Remove the needle, pull the crochet gently to stretch it and trim the end.

## Blocking

Crochet can tend to curl, so to make flat pieces stay flat you may need to block them. Pin the piece out to the correct size and shape on an ironing board or some soft foam mats (such as the ones sold as children's play mats). Spray with cold water, or cover with a cloth and press or steam gently (depending on the type of yarn—always follow the care instructions for the yarn you are using). Allow to dry completely before unpinning and removing from the board or mats.

For the flat crocheted elements for the wreaths and garlands in chapter 3, follow the same process but use ironing spray starch. Allow to dry for a day before attaching the elements to your wreath or garland. You will find that taking the time to block and stiffen each piece will make a huge difference to the finished effect of your work.

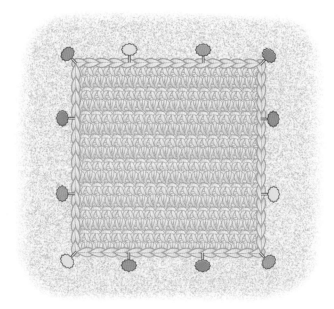

## Making an oversewn seam

An oversewn join gives a nice flat seam and is the simplest and most common joining technique.

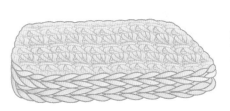

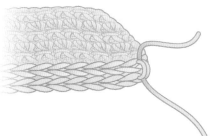

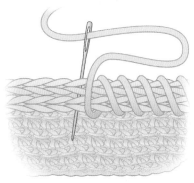

**1** Thread a yarn sewing needle with the yarn you're using in the project. Place the pieces to be joined with right sides together.

**2** Insert the needle in one corner in the top loops of the stitches of both pieces and pull up the yarn, leaving a tail of about 2in (5cm). Go into the same place with the needle and pull up the yarn again; repeat two or three times to secure the yarn at the start of the seam.

**3** Join the pieces together by taking the needle through the loops at the top of corresponding stitches on each piece to the end. Fasten off the yarn at the end, as in step 2.

## Making a single crochet seam

With a single crochet seam you join two pieces together using a crochet hook and working a single crochet stitch through both pieces, instead of sewing them together with a tail of yarn and a yarn sewing needle. This makes a quick and strong seam and gives a slightly raised finish to the edging. For a less raised seam, follow the same basic technique, but work each stitch in slip stitch rather than single crochet.

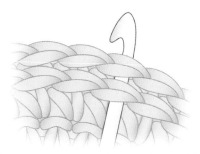

**1** Start by lining up the two pieces with wrong sides together. Insert the hook in the top 2 loops of the stitch of the first piece, then into the corresponding stitch on the second piece.

**2** Complete the single crochet stitch as normal and continue on the next stitches as directed in the pattern. This gives a raised effect if the single crochet stitches are made on the right side of the work.

**3** You can work with the wrong side of the work facing (with the pieces right side facing) if you don't want this effect and it still creates a good strong join.

## Surface crochet

Surface crochet is a simple way to add extra decoration to a finished item, working slip stitches over the surface of the fabric.

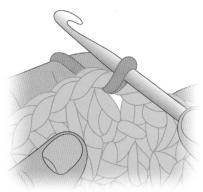

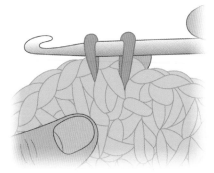

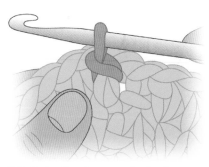

**1** Using a contrast yarn, make a slip knot (see page 79). Holding the yarn with the slip knot behind the work and the hook in front, insert the hook between two stitches from front to the back, and catch the slip knot behind the work with the hook. Draw the slip knot back through, so there is 1 loop on the hook at the front of the work.

**2** Insert the hook between the next 2 stitches, yarn over hook, and draw a loop through to the front. You will now have 2 loops on the hook.

**3** Pull the first loop on the hook through the second loop to complete the first slip stitch on the surface of the work.

Repeat steps 2 and 3 to make the next slip stitch. To join two ends with an invisible join, cut the yarn and thread onto a yarn needle. Insert the needle up through the last stitch, into the first stitch as if you were crocheting it, then into the back loop of the previous stitch. Fasten off on the wrong side.

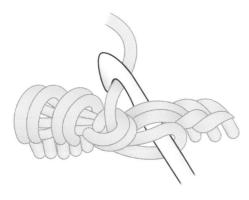

## Crab stitch

This is simply single crochet worked backward to give a twisted edge. Crab stitch spreads the edge slightly, so there's no need to increase to turn a corner. If a straight edge flutes, either miss the occasional stitch or use a smaller hook.

Do not turn the work at the end of the last row. Insert the hook in the last stitch to the right, yarn over hook, and pull through to make 2 loops twisted on the hook. Yarn over hook again and pull through making 1 loop on the hook. Repeat in the stitches along the edge or in row ends if necessary.

## Making a French knot

Bring the needle up from the back of the fabric to the front. Wrap the yarn two or three times around the tip of the needle, then reinsert the needle at the point where it first emerged, holding the wrapped yarn with the thumbnail of your non-stitching hand, and pull the needle all the way through. The wraps will form a knot on the surface of the crocheted fabric.

## Lazy daisy stitch

This stitch creates individual "chain links" that can be used to create "petals."

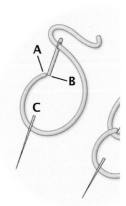

**1** Bring the needle up on the surface of the crocheted fabric at A. Take it back down at B, next to the point at which it emerged. Bring the needle back up directly below at C, looping the yarn under the tip of the needle. Draw up to tighten the loop on the surface of the fabric.

**2** When you've made the loop, insert the needle over the loop of the yarn to hold the loop down.

## Crochet stitch conversion chart

Crochet stitches are worked in the same way in both the USA and the UK, but the stitch names are not the same and identical names are used for different stitches. On the right is a list of the US terms used in this book, and the equivalent UK terms.

| US TERM | UK TERM |
| --- | --- |
| single crochet (sc) | double crochet (dc) |
| half double crochet (hdc) | half treble (htr) |
| double crochet (dc) | treble (tr) |
| treble (tr) | double treble (dtr) |
| double treble (dtr) | triple treble (trtr) |
| gauge | tension |
| yarn over hook (yoh) | yarn round hook (yrh) |

## Making a wreath

There are a wide range of wreaths available to buy, either online, in hobby stores or from a florist's, but it's also easy to make your own. For a wreath approximately 12in (30cm) in diameter when finished, you will need two 1¾oz (50g) packs of raffia and a roll of florist's wire. This method gives a very lightweight base that can be molded to the shape that you want. Raffia can be purchased either online or from hobby stores and it comes in a range of different colors.

Begin by taking the lengths of raffia out of the packets and carefully teasing the strands into long, straight lengths. Take one of the lengths and carefully attach the florist's wire tightly around one end to secure it. Begin twisting the raffia and the wire together, working your way down the length of raffia and wrapping the wire tightly around it as you twist.

As you work your way along the raffia you will find that it will become a little thinner as you get toward the end of the strand. At this point bring in the next length of raffia and carry on in the same way until you have combined both lengths of raffia into one long length. Add extra wire if there are parts that seem to need extra support. Trim all along the length of raffia to neaten, then secure the ends together with florist's wire to make a ring shape.

When attaching the crochet elements to your wreath, it's best to use a hot glue gun.

## Hanging garlands and wreaths

Hanging up a garland or displaying a wreath is such a quick way to add an instant change to your home décor, whether it's to welcome in a new season or to add decoration for festivals and celebrations. Garlands work particularly well hung below a mantelpiece or shelf, whether it's above a fireplace, in a bedroom, or even in the kitchen. They work equally well strung along bannisters of a staircase—and if you are lucky enough to have a house full of beams, the world is your oyster! Wreaths are very versatile and can be hung anywhere and everywhere, from a wall, to a door, to a gate. They also work equally well as stand-alone ornaments positioned on a shelf, mantelpiece, or dressing table.

I find the best way to secure a garland is by attaching a small hanging loop, made with either string or thin wire, at the back at each end. If your garland is divided into swags, just add further loops where needed to support the shape.

The hanging loop for a wreath can be hidden away at the back by attaching a loop of string or wire. Alternatively, the loop can be very much a part of the design, perhaps worked in coordinating ribbon and big enough to be seen over the top of the wreath.

## Storage

Wreaths and garlands can be stored by wrapping them in acid-free tissue paper and carefully packing them into a box.

## Abbreviations

| | |
|---|---|
| **alt** | alternat(e)ing |
| **approx.** | approximately |
| **beg** | beginning |
| **BLO** | back loop only |
| **ch** | chain |
| **cm** | centimeter(s) |
| **cont** | continu(e)ing |
| **dc** | double crochet |
| **dec** | decreas(e)ing |
| **dtr** | double treble |
| **foll** | follow(s)ing |
| **FP** | front post |
| **FPdc** | front post double crochet |
| **g** | gram(mes) |
| **hdc** | half double crochet |
| **in** | inch(es) |
| **inc** | increas(e)ing |
| **m** | meter(s) |
| **MB** | make bobble |
| **mm** | millimeter(s) |
| **MP** | make picot |
| **oz** | ounce(s) |
| **PM** | place marker |
| **prev** | previous |

| | |
|---|---|
| **rem** | remaining |
| **rep** | repeat |
| **RS** | right side |
| **sc** | single crochet |
| **sc2tog** | single crochet 2 stitches together |
| **sl st** | slip stitch |
| **st(s)** | stitch(es) |
| **tog** | together |
| **tr** | treble |
| **WS** | wrong side |
| **yd** | yards |
| **yoh** | yarn over hook |
| **[ ]** | work section between square brackets number of times stated * asterisk indicates beginning of repeated section of pattern |
| **\*** | asterisk indicates beginning of repeated section of pattern |

## Suppliers

We cannot cover all stockists here, so please explore the local yarn stores and online retailers in your own country.

If you wish to substitute a different yarn for the one recommended in the pattern, try the Yarnsub website for suggestions: www.yarnsub.com.

**USA**

**LoveCrafts**
Online sales
www.lovecrafts.com

**Knitting Fever Inc.**
www.knittingfever.com

**WEBS**
www.yarn.com

**Jo-Ann Fabric and Craft Stores**
Yarn and craft supplies
www.joann.com

**Michaels**
Craft supplies
www.michaels.com

**UK**

**LoveCrafts**
Online sales
www.lovecrafts.com

**Wool**
Yarn, hooks
Store in Bath
+44 (0)1225 469144
www.woolbath.co.uk

**Wool Warehouse**
Online sales
www.woolwarehouse.co.uk

**Laughing Hens**
Online sales
Tel: +44 (0) 1829 740903
www.laughinghens.com

**John Lewis**
Yarn and craft supplies
Telephone numbers of stores on website
www.johnlewis.com

**Hobbycraft**
Yarns, twig wreath bases, and raffia
www.hobbycraft.co.uk

**Australia**

**Black Sheep Wool 'n' Wares**
Retail store and online
Tel: +61 (0)2 6779 1196
www.blacksheepwool.com.au

**Sun Spun**
Retail store (Canterbury, Victoria) and online
Tel: +61 (0)3 9830 1609
www.sunspun.com.au

# Index

## Acknowledgments

With many thanks to the team at CICO Books for helping me
to put together this introduction to crochet. As always, every
care has been taken to ensure a beautiful finished product,
from the styling to the wonderful photography and the detailed
layout of each and every page. Thank you for allowing me
to create another book that I couldn't be prouder of.